Adult ~~Attachment~~ ~~and~~ psychotherapy

D1477460

Adult Personality Growth in Psychotherapy

Mardi J. Horowitz, M.D.

Distinguished Professor of Psychiatry
University of California San Francisco, CA, USA

CAMBRIDGE
UNIVERSITY PRESS

CAMBRIDGE
UNIVERSITY PRESS

University Printing House, Cambridge CB2 8BS, United Kingdom

Cambridge University Press is part of the University of Cambridge.

It furthers the University's mission by disseminating knowledge in the pursuit of education, learning and research at the highest international levels of excellence.

www.cambridge.org
Information on this title: www.cambridge.org/9781107532960

First published 2016

Printed in the United Kingdom by Clays, St Ives plc

A catalogue record for this publication is available from the British Library

Library of Congress Cataloging-in-Publication Data
Horowitz, Mardi Jon, 1934– , author.
Adult personality growth in psychotherapy / Mardi J. Horowitz.
Cambridge ; New York : Cambridge University Press, 2016. |
Includes bibliographical references and index.
LCCN 2016003556 | ISBN 9781107532960 (paperback)
| MESH: Self Concept | Psychotherapy | Identification (Psychology) | Emotions | Adult
LCC RC454 | NLM WM 460.5.P3 | DDC 616.89–dc23
LC record available at http://lccn.loc.gov/2016003556

ISBN 978-1-107-53296-0 Paperback

....

Contents

Preface   *page* vii
Acknowledgments   viii

1. Achieving personality growth in psychotherapy   1

Section I.   Self-organization   13
2. Self-organization   15
3. Identity functioning and self-states   27
4. Possibilities for change in self-narratives   37

Section II.   Relationships   51
5. Changing relationship patterns   53
6. Advancing relationship capacities   65
7. Improving maladaptive patterns in sexual relationships   77

Section III. Control and emotional regulation   89
8. Control of unconscious emotional potentials   91
9. Defensive styles   99
10. Emotional avoidance maneuvers   109

References   125
Glossary of terms   134
Index   137

Preface

Psychotherapy for personality growth aims towards augmenting a sense of identity, enriching relationships, and enhancing control of emotion. Integration of these key factors requires that a person learn to modify a narrative of characteristics of self in the present as articulated to the past and having future goals. Therapy towards these ends changes mental structures through both conscious and unconscious processing.

New modes of thinking about self and others means navigating emotional waters that have seemed turbulent. Safety in that course occurs by developing a therapeutic alliance, having frank conversations about dangers, and exploring new ways of coping with them rather than avoiding them. While important, insight is not the sole road to such adaptive changes. New relationship experiences can also lead to significant and enduring changes in attitudes, intentions, and expectations.

This book uses contemporary theories from cognitive and psychodynamic sciences, especially a modern understanding of the operation of schemas and emotional-control processes. Clinicians operating within cognitive-behavioral therapy frameworks, especially, may value this component of complexity in case formulation. Clinicians trained in psychodynamic therapy may value the specific emphasis on techniques to promote present moments of learning.

My approach includes attention to how a clinician can understand and modify symptoms, problems, and pathogenic feelings and thoughts. It also addresses how a therapist can increase a patient's capacity for resilience, strength, and creativity. I do not argue that what I present is altogether new. Instead, I combine known elements from many sources while trying my best for brevity, clarity, and illustration. I believe the results are consistent with modern neuroscience, developmental psychology, and socio-cultural understanding.

Change involves the modification of configurations of meanings about identity as nested in attachments. That is why this book will progressively examine and illustrate layers of self-beliefs and narratives. This is the reason I begin with a section of three chapters focused on identity and its variation across different states of mind.

The second section, consisting of three chapters, centers on relationship patterns and capacities. The final section of three chapters examines emotional control.

Acknowledgments

My academic home has been the University of California San Francisco and I thank all the patients, trainees, and faculty colleagues who have made my work over decades rewarding and stimulating. Colleagues in the MacArthur Program on Conscious and Unconscious Mental Processes, which I directed, and the staff in Chicago were also immensely supportive. The National Institute of Mental Health supported much of the research on which the knowledge in this book is based, and psychotherapy research colleagues around the world have also made it all possible. My wife, Renee Binder, M.D., is also President of the American Psychiatric Association, and Past Chairman of UCSF Psychiatry. In addition to support throughout, we have studied the key issues of where does psychotherapy go next, in relation to diagnoses and formulations.

Zack Vanderbilt did major work in getting all aspects of the manuscript together. He contributed important feedback on the ideas and how they were presented. I am proud of his work. Marilyn Spoja and Bente Mirow helped refine the writing. Then Drs. Kat Lopez, Nadia Taylor, Paul Elizondo, Wendy Feng, Adam Goldyne, Chelsea Young, Tracy Foose, Serina Dean, and Alice Huang were the most vital readers who led to clarity and augmentation.

Achieving personality growth in psychotherapy

Personality is a combination of qualities that endure and yet slowly evolve. Psychotherapy can modify existing personality characteristics that cause social and occupational dysfunction as well as personal suffering. This process of modifying personality structure involves new learning experiences and can be supported by a deeper understanding of the patient's relationships with the therapist and others, in addition to an appreciation of the self's inherent complexity. The benefits of personality growth include a more coherent identity; increased capacity for richer, deeper, and more enduring relationships; and improved emotional control, including tolerance for negative feelings such as fear and sadness.

Psychotherapy can assist in personality growth when a therapist makes careful observations, formulates the multiple underlying causes of salient problems, and uses techniques that promote new learning opportunities. Each chapter in this book will begin with several observations, followed by their proposed formulations, and will conclude with an illustration of relevant techniques. This first chapter provides an overview of observations, formulations, and techniques utilizing a case example to illustrate each of these three elements, followed by a discussion of the general principles of technique.

Observation

Observations are made based on the patient's report of conscious personal and interpersonal experiences including complaints and symptoms, signs that are observed during therapeutic sessions, and the therapist's own emotional response to the patient. The therapist may observe deficiencies in certain general capacities, such as difficulty in thinking clearly or in separating fantasy from reality. Observations are also made regarding how a patient responds to the therapist's interventions. If, for example, a patient rejects a comment the therapist offers, an observation might be made about the nature of the rejection.

Such an observation could then inform a formulation of the case. In considering the quality of the observation, the therapist might ask him/herself if the comment was rejected because it was not attuned to the patient in some way, in need of revision, or perhaps evocative of strong feelings that the patient wants to avoid. A variety of observations combine to contribute to the formulation of what is happening in the present therapy moment.

Silver

The case of Silver will be used as an example of moving from observation to formulation and technique.

Silver was a 31-year-old unmarried man when he sought treatment for anxiety symptoms. He had periods in which his tense muscles, sweaty palms, sense of dread, and ruminative worry significantly interfered with his work. He also had difficulties with feeling inferior and maintaining intimate personal relationships, both of which caused him distress. He was diagnosed with Generalized Anxiety Disorder, but his problems seemed closely related to long-standing and personality challenges regarding identity and relationships. A differential diagnosis of Narcissistic Personality Disorder with compulsive and dysphoric features was considered.

Silver had worked for several years in lower management at a large corporation. About six months prior to his presentation for treatment, he had been promoted. His increasing responsibilities involved more frequent and important interactions with the people whom he supervised as well as with those who supervised him. In addition, as the scope of his work widened, he had to cooperate more and more with his peers. The interactions, though desirable, increased his tension and anxiety.

Silver hoped to develop cooperative partnerships with his workplace peers, yet he felt uneasy and suspicious that his colleagues might act in competitive ways that would interfere with his chances for advancement in the company. If others wanted to cooperate with him on a project, Silver felt edgy and would withdraw from them, feeling more anxious because he was unsure what the right or wrong behaviors would be. He would fluctuate back and forth, anxiously approaching coworkers, and then withdrawing from them for fear of embarrassment.

Silver had recently dated a woman for three months, during which time they had satisfying sexual experiences. When Silver asked her to move in with him, she ended their connection firmly but kindly, telling him that he was "not right for her." He felt that she viewed herself as superior to him, and did not see him worthy of domestic partnership or marriage. Since this experience Silver had dated sporadically, but felt that the women he dated were inferior to what he expected for himself.

Silver desired both friendship and intimacy with a woman, but seldom achieved either. Whenever he sought to deepen a relationship, he ended up feeling rejected and unworthy. As a result, he tended to stay away from people. He felt very alert to possible signs of scorn, rejection, or exploitation by others.

In discussing an exploratory and possibly open-ended course of psychotherapy with him, his goals were clarified. He wanted to have more pride and confidence in the work he produced, and to be able to share more with his work peers. He also wanted more close friends and intimate relationships. He even desired to get married, but he was seldom able to feel relaxation and mutuality with women.

As a result of the limited relationships, both at his work and in his love life, Silver often felt lonely and sad. He loved to listen to music, and it helped him to ease his distress. He drank alcohol in moderation, but wanted to reduce that, as it seemed to him like an escape that could lead to further trouble.

During the evaluation interviews, he seemed engaging, clear, and motivated to gain a better self-understanding. Therapy began as weekly sessions, sometimes twice a week. About a month into the psychotherapy, after the opening minutes of each session, he seemed to slump down and draw back. In this apathetic state, he might flip-flop in his attitude toward therapy, stating that he felt unsure about being there, and spent much time indecisively and abstractly deliberating on whether therapy could help him in any way.

After perhaps ten minutes in this state, he would usually rouse himself and try to come out of his shell. He would speak on topics concerning his work and relationships until he became more anxious, and then he would slump into what seemed like a restorative mood in which he was almost aloof to the therapist. He expressed feelings, yet also made efforts to suppress them. The feelings, flickering over his face, were often expressed only briefly and then masked. They appeared to be a mixture of self-disgust, sadness, and fear—a state of mind of mixed emotions in which he had difficulty connecting feelings to ideas.

Observations of Silver included his self-report of anxiety and problematic relationships socially and at work. He avoided people to reduce states of tension and sweaty palms, but the avoidance led to loneliness. During sessions the therapist observed that Silver exhibited tense facial muscles and avoidance of eye contact. These signs decreased in intensity and frequency after the first weeks. The therapist noted his own reactions during sessions. He became hyper-alert when Silver seemed to tense up, and bored when Silver seemed to drone on without communicating directly and honestly.

Formulation

Formulation in therapies for personality growth usually moves from a surface observation towards the delineation of repetitive and maladaptive interpersonal patterns. These patterns are rarely apparent during the first evaluation and early phases of therapy. As therapy progresses and more information is gathered, the therapist can begin to infer how and why patterns repeat themselves in spite of unfortunate consequences. Additionally, as time goes by, the therapist develops hypotheses as to what may be causing blunting of possibilities for self-actualization and satisfaction.

The macro-formulations of the whole case begin with mini-formulations of what is going on in the present moment. In going from surface observations and disclosures to deeper meaning structures, a therapist may utilize a framework called **configurational analysis** (Horowitz, 2005; Horowitz, Marmar et al., 1984; Horowitz, 1997, 2005; Horowitz and Ells, 1997, 2005). In this framework, the therapist begins by analyzing the states of mind in which the observable phenomena do and do not appear. The therapist then considers the emotions that may lead to changes in mental states, such as into defensive states or disorganized states of extreme distress. These are labeled "topics of concern."

Then one examines whether the emotions and state changes can be grouped into "views of the self in relationship with others" and "self-criticisms." These enduring and slowly changing attitudes will be called person schemas. The steps of such configurational analyses are: **states, topics of concern, and person schemas**.

States

After selecting certain phenomena for attention, the therapist and patient may consider the states in which they occur, as well as those states in which they do not occur. Silver's sweaty palms occurred in a *tense* state of mind. This tense state then contrasted with his *apathetic* or aloof state of mind, which was achieved and stabilized when he was able to avoid others either by working alone in his office cubicle or by delving into solitary interests and hobbies.

Silver desired a state he termed *happiness*. Silver differentiated happiness from the state that he sometimes experienced when in great distress, which was a depressed state of feeling that "everything is worthless." Over the course of therapy, states of shame and anger were eventually uncovered, neither of which were recognized at the time of first formulation. Although some states occur in therapy sessions, wider ranges are reported from self-observation in other contexts such as while at work or with family or friends.

Emotional regulation is central to this analytic step of conceptualizing states of mind as comprising a patient's repertoire. Emotional regulation can range from under-control to over-modulation. For example, repetitive phenomena such as angry expressions can occur in well-modulated states, in explosive under-controlled states, or in blunted over-controlled states. The therapist's attention should include not only the angry feelings, but also how the anger varies in intensity, associated ideas, and level of control.

On one occasion during Silver's therapy, the therapist was surprised when Silver entered a state of under-modulated shame, cringing into the recesses of his chair, looking furtively and frightened at the therapist while blurting out something like "I am such a wreck." Silver quickly recovered, but over the course of many sessions the state of searing shame recurred as he became more exploratory of his ideas and feelings. Triggers of this state were observed and became topics of attention.

In general, several questions may help the therapist formulate mental states, determine topics of concern, and develop person schemas. These questions are:

When and why do state transitions occur?
Do certain topics trigger the patient's entry into distressing states?
Are there states of mind during which the patient seems to experience or present alternative identities?

Topics of concern

Transitions into under- over-controlled states may occur with the emergence of certain topics that bring up emotions that are difficult for the patient, and perhaps even the therapist, to experience. A topic may return again and again because it is important, conflictual, and unresolved. It may be avoided for a while before it returns as a topic to be discussed.

Silver might, in therapy, be in a conversational, well-modulated state, but then shift to either an under- or over-controlled avoidant state when confronting the topic of feeling lonely. In a state of safety, Silver was able to discuss this topic and relate incidents of anticipated or actual rejections of friendly conversations at work, or of asking a woman to go on a date. Some stories involved his own ineptitude, which led to him entering an intense, degraded, and shame-filled state.

The therapist observed that Silver expected his overtures to lead to a response of rejection, and that this anticipation also contributed to the tension he experienced when he forced himself to approach others. Thus, while engaging others with as much charm as he could muster, Silver was also anxiously expecting their possible lack of interest.

His hypervigilance for rejection often superseded his desire for intimacy, prompting Silver to wall himself off from others and enter his calmer but unsatisfying state of apathy and aloofness. This helped Silver regulate both his experience of tension and his sense of degradation, but it also left him lonely. When that became a depressive state, Silver would once again venture to connect with others, but the cyclic pattern described would unfold once again despite Silver's dearly held hope for a different experience.[1]

A therapist and a patient will likely recognize only certain aspects of salient topics before understanding all of the submerged meanings. A therapist's notation of these repetitive behaviors and themes may flesh out formulations.

Avoidances are important to observe. At times, the patient may veer away from a certain topic, perhaps inhibiting or distorting certain concepts. An important aim is to help the patient feel safer and more in control of what topics can be addressed, and what emotions can be more fully experienced. One way Silver avoided entry into the potentially under-modulated state of shame was to focus attention on the other person's shortcomings: he would deny any desire to make a deeper connection with such a person, and judge them as an unsatisfactory potential companion. If there had been an argument, Silver presented the incident implying that the other person was at fault.

---

[1] Wachtel (1993) points out the irony in these patterns, in which, "the situation that the patient ends up in is precisely the one he is trying to avoid. He does not *aim* for the consequences he encounters; he produces them despite—yet because of—his vigorous efforts to prevent them … The irony in what ensues lies in how, by the very act of carrying out that intention, the patient contributes to the outcome he is trying to avoid" (pp. 23–24).

In addition to observations, the therapist may develop certain questions. Do certain topics feel stressful on recollection, or repeatedly lead to under-modulated states? Are certain topics dismissed or distorted by the use of defensive maneuvers to down-regulate emotion? Does the patient use a habitual emotional control style to avoid certain topics?

Person schemas

Person schemas operate unconsciously in order to organize the combination of internal knowledge and external sensations into thoughts and feelings. By the time it is possible to conceptualize this deep level of case formulation, the therapist and the patient, most likely together, will have noted particularly problematic states. As the therapist observes which topic shifts lead to that state, the therapist can look for various habitual *self-concepts and relationship attitudes* in each state. Eventually, the origins of these attitudes can be illuminated.

Person schemas are often dyadic; the self-other relationship models that inform thoughts about difficult topics are expressed through therapeutic dialogue. Such a model is illustrated by Silver's statement: "I am too weak, I just caved in when he said. . ." These kinds of statements reveal self-concepts and social attitudes.

For example, Silver might meet a new person and expect them to arrogantly disparage him because they are older, stronger, more expensively dressed, and/or in a bigger office. Silver's *transference* feelings about the therapist gave insight into his person schemas. For example, he expected the therapist to degrade him when he confessed to incompetent behaviors or could not clearly express his feelings. Through the therapeutic relationship, he came to learn that in reality the therapist might be kindly disposed, cooperative, and understanding of his experience, which undermined the automatic imposition of his unconscious relationship model that organized his thinking. By becoming aware of what was real rather than habitual, he gained new experiences in therapy and learned new role relationship models.

Once conceptualized, attitudes can be investigated in terms of how they formed and habitually repeated in the past. What was implicit and procedural can be elevated to verbal, declarative, and explicit statements. That can lead to a deeper understanding of how and why a certain maladaptive pattern in interpersonal relationships is repeated, and ultimately how to forge a new pattern. Habitual beliefs can be challenged with new cognitive processes that reflect a more positive outlook.

Technique

With Silver, the therapist promoted a shared experiencing of Silver's thoughts and feelings. He provided clear labels for Silver to use in identifying the feelings and attitudes that might trigger entry into a tense and anxious *state*. He did so by repeating what Silver said with tentative words for expressing emotions more clearly in their conversations.

Labeling these *topical* triggers helped Silver stabilize more centered states and communicate his feelings to the therapist. This process helped the therapist attend to Silver's shifting states, as well as the beliefs about self and others that were expressed therein. Moments in which Silver sought to minimize his negative emotions were called to his attention. The therapist then used both clarification and interpretation to engage Silver in an exploration of the *core relationship patterns* that informed his shifting sense of self and his expectations of others.

Silver and the therapist discussed various ways to understand and handle rejection. They explored new ways of connecting with others that might be more socially effective. The therapist began to challenge the irrational components of Silver's self-concept of unworthiness. The therapist encouraged more rational views of himself and more development of skills. This helped Silver integrate existing positive beliefs about himself and his relationships, which led to the adoption of combinations of beliefs that reflected a more realistic, continuous sense of self-efficacy.

The case of Silver illustrated how, in the middle phase of therapy, maladaptive attitudes about identity and relationship can be clarified and challenged. Self-concepts and self-judgments are often found to be discordant or irrational in that they neither reflect a patient's current situation, nor do they accurately appraise personal potential. The process of change involves learning to re-focus attention and reappraise old beliefs. Then therapy conversations can create new plans and improve self-regulation.

General principles of technique

General principles include creating a sense of safety, tactfully redirected or deepening attention, observing for signs of progress or stagnation, and containing emotionality as deeper attitudes emerge.

Safety and emotional containment in a therapeutic alliance

Negative emotions often feel dangerous; they can lead to dreaded states of mind. Both the therapist and the patient will find that the therapy processes can proceed well when **safety** is established, full expression is encouraged, and hope is present. This means that the therapist seeks to understand the meanings beyond the patient's immediate words. Such readiness involves going beyond the patient's story into subtle meanings and stances. The right frame of mind for the therapist could be taking an equidistant position on various parts of the patient's conflict so that all parts can be expressed.

The idea of the therapist's neutrality has been revised in the years since Freud used a free association method to encourage awareness of repressed memories, fantasies, ideas, and feelings.[2] A more fruitful frame of mind is to listen for possibly conflicting concepts that arise in the patient and in the therapist's own reactive mind. The patient may be explicitly asked to explore emotions and meanings thoughtfully, instead of arriving at hasty judgments, which over time can move toward more holistic solutions.

Focusing attention on a topic

In a therapy environment, patient and therapist select a *topic as the focus for their joint attention*. The patient usually generates this topic in the opening period of the session. The therapist listens for a potentially useful theme to emerge and follows its thread through the patient's discourse. Eventually, the topic is refined as one that contains dilemmas or conflicts that are problematic for the patient.

As the patient tells stories about what has happened and caused them distress, the therapist aims to gradually help the patient establish reasonable *cause-and-effect sequences*. Sometimes it helps to compare and contrast different outcomes of a pertinent conflict, such as best-case, worst-case, and most likely scenarios. This contrast can help the patient think realistically and reduce exaggerations and minimizations.

Meanwhile, the therapist watches for defenses that serve as obstacles to understanding. These emotional control processes act to prevent anticipated dangers and in doing so often operate at the pre-conscious levels of information processing. This means that a patient may be unaware of the presence and function of these avoidance operations, in addition to the thoughts and feelings that are being suppressed. Interventions that help with fuller and safer emotional expression can lead to clarification of suppressed emotions, and perhaps also to the modification of maladaptive inhibitions, avoidance patterns, and unintentional "blind spots."

The process of expressing a richer narrative on a difficult topic will lead to feelings embedded in, and in part caused by, *repeated maladaptive attitudes*. As these attitudes are clarified, it may be helpful to trace the routes of their development. This may involve expressing childhood memories and fantasies. Past traumas can be addressed to develop new self-narratives.

Psychotherapy involves both learning and unlearning. However, it is important to understand that unlearning does not mean erasure: although models of past self-other configurations endure unconsciously, they can be rendered latent by activating and developing more adaptive views of self and other. This process can be fostered by new, mutually authentic attachments. The evolution of an effective and realistic *therapeutic alliance* is one such attachment. Modifying habitual

---

[2] For an emotion-focused take on neutrality, see Beuchler (2008). Beuchler has emphasized the utility, as well as the limits, of the therapist's cultivation of a state of curiosity. Beuchler suggests that this state often enables the therapist to help the patient maintain, or more accurately, regain the emotional equilibrium that is crucial to the therapeutic process. In this way, she follows Schafer's (1983) and Greenberg's (1986) positions that neutrality (in the sense of equidistance between parts of a conflict) involves a state of being that affects the interpersonal field, in addition to a set of behaviors that avoids harsh critical judgments (Horowitz, 2013).

defensive styles and automatic avoidances are often necessary in order to engage in the corrective experiences that can occur in therapy.

Evaluating progress in therapy

Part of the observation, formulation, and technique revision that the therapist utilizes in different phases of treatment involves continuous evaluations of how the therapy is progressing. Symptoms and problematic states can be considered in terms of intensity and frequency over time. Although distress may temporarily increase with fuller emotional expression, it should improve gradually over time and give rise to increased life satisfaction.

States of mind ideally become easier to modulate, leading to more confidence and spontaneity. *Topics* that have been too traumatic to contemplate should move towards completion and a sense of mastery. Concepts of self and other may become progressively more realistic, *person schemas* may be reconfigured, and social actions may become more effective.

The therapist may ask him- or herself the following questions to assess progress:

- Is the patient gaining a greater ability to reflect on his or her own mental processes in a way that connects cognition and affect as opposed to defensive intellectualization or emotional flooding? Silver gradually learned more language for labeling his feelings and his states of mind, indicating progress.
- Is the patient learning more about how to understand more accurately and deeply the motivations, intentions, and attitudes of others? For Silver, the therapist's questions about what he thought the other person deserved in a particular social situation led to new insights and more realistic expectations.
- Is the patient learning cause-and-effect reasoning to anticipate the potential consequences of their own actions? Although Silver had always worried about disapproval by supervisors when he had to show his work, he became able to focus more on favorable outcomes and how to amplify their probability. He was able to map out in advance how he would handle scheduled interviews with his supervisors.
- Is the person gaining a greater sense of realistic self-confidence? Silver gradually gained pride from an enhanced capacity to engage his friend when on dates rather than giving in to his fears and withdrawing.

By focusing on personal meaning systems and specific plans of how to approach situations that cause distress or impairment, a patient may begin to: (1) develop more rational views and patterns of action (*i.e.*, become more realistic); (2) modify defensive styles (*e.g.*, to express even distressing emotions more safely); and (3) learn to use new rational views and behavior patterns to either counteract or contain irrational views or impulsive patterns. Small changes in these areas accrue and lead to larger and more difficult changes. As a patient tests for safety and finds it, he or she is likely to progressively confront more and more emotionally complex topics.

Bringing maladaptive patterns and dysfunctional thoughts to the patient's conscious awareness amplifies his or her learning about coping and relating.

At the level of conscious awareness, and in conversation with the therapist, the patient examines beliefs and goals that are usually intuited but not clearly verbalized or discussed with another person. The patient learns new conceptual skills to integrate discrepancies and contradictory views on the self and others.

Patients ideally develop new patterns of self-evaluation, as well as new ways to work with others, be productive, gain intimacy, improve caretaking functions, and regulate emotion. These capacities are planned and practiced to discover if they are more adaptive than past patterns. Focused attention and conscious thinking can be used to solve problems in life in general, as well as to address issues that have been dwelling within the patient as unconscious memories, fantasies, intentions, and expectations.

Conversations with a therapist help the patient advance in capacities for reflective *self-awareness*: reflecting on conscious thoughts expands a patient's awareness of possible choices in ways that lead towards better decisions. Long-standing dilemmas give way to solutions that are neither too ideal to realize, nor too catastrophic to contemplate.

As a sign of progress, Silver appeared to increase in his ability to use reflective thinking about himself during sessions. Many patients become more adept at integrating potentially conflicting threads of cognitive-affective experience by entertaining perspectives of the self and the other, while recognizing the limits of each perspective. By exercising mentalization, a patient can re-examine thoughts and feelings that occur in primary consciousness, and then clarify and modify them in a way that allows for greater tolerance of ambiguity, better affect regulation, and ultimately, a more stable and flexible sense of self in relation to others (Bateman & Fonagy, 2004; Fonagy, Gergely, Jurist, & Target, 2004; Fonagy & Target, 2006, 2000; Falkenstrom et al., 2007). In order for psychotherapy to achieve personality growth, patients must develop the ability to reflect on their own as well as others' mental states.

Containing emotional attitudes safely

The expectation within the *role-relationship model* of an adequate *therapeutic alliance* is that the therapist will help the patient safely contemplate fantasies, thoughts, and emotions the patient finds threatening. Additionally, the therapist will utilize professional expertise to maintain the therapeutic frame, even in the face of pressure from *transference* and *countertransference* feelings to do otherwise. This work facilitates the exploration of experiences that the patient may avoid outside of therapy, whether consciously or unconsciously, due to a fear of being overwhelmed by them.[3] Under these circumstances, person

---

[3] As I have described it here, the therapist's provision for the patient's expectations—which range from unconscious fantasies to explicitly articulated desires—encompasses both Bion's (1962, 1967) concept of the therapist's role as a container for the patient's unconscious projections of intolerable and unintegrated aspects of self and other, and Winnicott's (1972) concept of the therapeutic space as a holding environment.

schematizations for identity and relationships can be modified or augmented by corrective experiences.

Corrective experiences and conscious insight can unconsciously modify cognitive maps. Reflective awareness allows patients to assess their attitudes and devise new possibilities. They can compare alternate, possibly opposing plans, consider which potential outcome is preferable, and decide how to proceed. In such contemplations, a patient can sometimes merge conflicting views and goals to arrive at an adaptive compromise or a new harmony.

Just as crucially, a patient may be able to learn how to imagine the thoughts and feelings of others in a social situation. This act of empathy can begin to shift perspective sufficiently to engender new ways of being in a challenging interpersonal situation. This practice of reflective awareness, including an empathic response to others, underlies the ability to successfully implement newly formed plans for challenging situations.

Unconscious workings of the mind, which hum along in the background of conscious representation, contribute to the problem-solving capacity of reflective awareness. Unconscious cognitive maps are in turn affected by intentions and beliefs that arise from problem-solving trains of conscious thought (LeDoux, 1995). As pre-conscious anticipations operate below conscious representations, parallel channels of processing go on appraising what is happening in the present moment and the anticipated future. These combinations of information can be organized by different role-relationship models. That is, enduring person schemas from a person's previously established repertoire of self-other beliefs function to unite internal and external sources of information. One goal of this technique is to improve harmony in this repertoire.

Many people can learn to attend to and reflect on emotional cues, thereby representing in words as tools for thinking clearly some previously non-verbal expectations and intentions. By focusing reflective awareness in this way, patients can gain greater conscious access to the attitudes that emerge from their role-relationship models. This access to otherwise unconscious information can increase the flexibility of previously rigid attitudes in a process that is called **insight**. Insight, new plans for the future, and **corrective experiences** that occur without insight all contribute to personality growth in psychotherapy

Self-organization

Some patients come for therapy for problems in living and realize that they also are in search of a sense of coherence in self-organization. Many patients discuss identity in terms of their community connections and lack of them, and in terms of their relationships. However, conflicts, dissociations, and deficiencies involving self-concepts and self-appraisals are important to observe, formulate, and address in the use of techniques to promote change.

Identity-related issues are addressed in three chapters. Chapter two deals with levels of personality functioning. Chapter three focuses on degrees of control in varied self-states Chapter four deals with processes that can advance self-narratives towards realism.

Self-organization

As patient and therapist work together to review past events, current sense of identity, and future plans, they develop a more conscious self-narrative for the patient. They share observations of identity disturbances and beliefs about roles and capacities. The observations lead to formulations of current level of functioning and potential enhancements of self-organization. The therapist plans techniques for new learning that are likely to work with the current level of mental and social functioning. Progress is assessed by evolution of the patient's self-reflective capacities and a sense of increased authenticity and self-esteem. That completes the cycle back to observation, and the interaction of observing, formulating and intervening continues.

Understanding the patient's experience of self-regard, self-esteem, and self-monitoring is core to this process. Observation involves clarification of the varied self-states of an individual, especially those that are problematic. For example, the patient may present in a poised manner in early sessions, and then present a feeble posture and self-doubting dialogue in later sessions.

Formulation involves inferences about the nature of the patient's transitions between observed self-states in varied circumstances and roles. The patient who shifts explosively into the self-state that looks feeble is different from a patient who gradually gets into discussing a topic about which they feel weak, and then resume their postures and dialogue of poise. Smooth transitions occur with higher levels of self-organization, while explosive and major changes in self-presentation and self-experience occur with lower levels of functioning.

Such formulations lead the therapist to make trial interventions, then observe what works best in the present phase of therapy. In general, persons with more discord in self-organization will require simple, repetitive, clear, tactful and emotionally containing techniques of intervention. In contrast, patients at a higher level of self-organization can process more complex and developmentally reconstructive clarifications and interpretations of how maladaptive beliefs about the self may have developed (Horowitz, 2013, 2014; Wachtel, 2014; McWilliams, 2011; Young et al., 2006). By tolerating more complex statements from the therapist, the patient can make linkages and gain insight into a pattern across time frames (past, present, and anticipated future) and across social situations (significant personal relationships and the therapeutic relationship). With less complex statements that focus on a clear and immediate topic of concern, the therapist may avoid confusing a patient who, in current state, is functioning at a lower level of self-organization.

Observation

Therapists gain a sense of who they are dealing with. Some observations make the therapists say to themselves, jarringly, "who am I dealing with?" The observation of signs that leads to the jarring sense of personality variation within the individual patient's self-presentation has to do with several features. These features include the degree to which the therapist believes the patient is sharing with the therapist a sense of current reality, as opposed to irrational beliefs about the here and now, and the degree to which the patient has smoothness in emotional transition.

A patient may cry, but there is an observable difference between understandable tears and sudden, surprising sobbing. Dissociation may be observed as abrupt shifts in emotional state, in which the patient may act unaware of their dramatically different affect compared to only moments before. As an example, consider the same kind of therapist remark and two extremes of patient responsiveness to the remark. Suppose a therapist says to a patient, "I think you are still in some way angry at your mother." The patient says, "Hmm, I don't know. Let me think about that," and goes on to avoid the topic. Although this avoidance of discourse on the topic offered by the therapist could be a sign of defensiveness, or simply the therapist's inaccuracy, the response is not strange, discordant, or disjunctive.

In a different example, after the therapist says, "I think you are still in some way angry at your mother," the patient visibly stiffens, his face and voice change, and the therapist notes his own startle reaction as the patient becomes angry at the therapist. For several minutes the patient curses and uses bad names for what the therapist is "really like." Soon after, the patient composes himself and resumes the topic under discussion before the episode. He avoids the topic of hostility towards his mother that the therapist had expressed. The session ends normally.

In the next session, the therapist inquires, "I wonder what you remember about our last session." The patient asks, "What do you mean?" When the therapist remains silent and presents a calm countenance of acceptance and curiosity, the patient says, " Oh, I saw red at some point, but I don't remember what I said. I guess I got pretty angry, but whatever I may have said, that was not me. No. That's all I remember. What happened?" The patient seems reflective and the explosive hostility was largely forgotten. This response gives the impression of dissociation between the patient's self-states, and in one state the patient could not recall memories that might be available when in the other state.

In addition to asking the patient to recall what happened, it may be helpful to ask more specific questions, such as:

- As that was going on, did you feel not quite yourself?
- During that moment, did you experience your body in a strange way?
- When you recall that, how did you picture yourself in your mind's eye?
- So your reaction was thus and so, and how did you evaluate yourself after you did that?
- Why did your acquaintance tell you that she thought you were too changeable and unpredictable, what specifics might she have had in mind?

Formulation

The different self-states observed in a patient may be formulated as the patient unconsciously activating various elements from a repertoire of *self-schemas*. Different self-schemas may lead to different postures and mental pictures of the self, as well as different ways of feeling, thinking, and interpreting perceptions. Sometimes these schemas operate independently, as if they lack associations with one another. In some instances, this lack of association may imply lower levels of self-organization. In other instances, the dissociation is a product of current stress and a return to a higher level of functioning will occur quickly.

In high levels of personality functioning, a person's multiple self-schemas are organized into *supraordinate configurations*. In patients who are vulnerable to dissociative identity experiences, self-schemas may not be integrated into coherent meaning structures. Meaning structures are complex connectivities between many levels and kinds of information that can be coordinated in cognitive processing. An example of hierarchical nesting of elements in overall self-organization is illustrated in Figure 2.1. Part of formulation is to judge how well this harmonization has occurred thus far in development.

Self-schemas are inferred as part of a larger model of relationship. *Role relationship models* embed the self in a *cognitive map* that contains attributes of the self and of the other person. If self is configured as a victim, then dyadic completion tends towards appraising the other person as the aggressor in a relationship (Grey et al., 2014). In addition, role-relationship models include a *transactive scenario*, in which the individual expects their actions to evoke the other person's response, and in turn the individual expects to have a reaction to their response. *Desired scenarios* tend to activate positive emotions, whereas *dreaded scenarios* may lead to negative emotions, including self-criticism, shame, and guilt.

In an unfamiliar situation with no basis for expectations from the other person, the preconscious mind tries out possible models. The person is pre-consciously

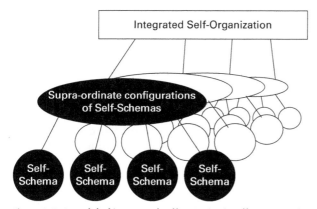

Figure 2.1 A model of integrated self-organization (from Horowitz, 2014)

looking through available organizing principles for the ideal lens to determine the possibilities and probabilities of various interactions with the other person. Those with an impoverished repertoire of role relationship models, or with limited social intelligence, are less likely to accurately perceive an interpersonal interaction (LeDoux, 1995; Panskeep and Biven, 2013; Porges, 2011).

In order to distinguish between a stress-induced dip in functioning and an established personality structure, the therapist formulates the patient's current *level of integration*. Observations are pooled into inferences of fuzzy categories from high to low levels of integration in a patient's self-organization. These categories can be conceptualized as levels that descend from harmonious connectivities to fragmented units in discord. The lowest level may lead to expressive styles in which the patient feels depersonalized, empty, and even psychotic states. Middle levels reflect feelings such as mildly conflicted, vulnerable, and disturbed. Relevant observations are summarized for this important range of levels of function in Table 2.1.

Table 2.1 Levels of integration of self-organization (from Horowitz, 2014)

Level	Description
Harmonious	Internal desires, needs, frustrations, impulses, choices, and values are appraised as "of the self." Realistic pros and cons are examined to reach choices of rational action and restraint. Grounded in self, one views others as separate people with their own intentions, expectations, and emotional reactions. Perspectives on relationships approximate social realities. Past and present views of self and relationships are integrated, allowing a sense of constancy and modification of ambivalence. State transitions are smooth, appropriate, and adroit. Warm and caring relationships are maintained over time in spite of episodic frustrations. Emotional governance prevents out-of-control states.
Mildly Conflicted	While good-enough relationships are formed in his or her closest work and intimate affiliations, the person displays states that contain varied intentions, manifesting as conflicting approach and distancing tendencies. On examination, these alternations are based on fluctuating attitudes about self in the relationship. Most commonly, fears of rejection may limit warm and caring attachments to others, or fears of subordination limit high levels of cooperation. The person appraises self with a variety of critical judgments: some too harsh, some too lax. State transitions occur between positive and negative moods, but the shifts in states are remembered and tempered by some understanding rather than being dissociated, or appearing to others as surprising emergence of alternative selves.
Vulnerable	A sense of self-regard deteriorates under stress, criticism, and increased pressures to perform. To protect from feelings of inferiority or enfeeblement, grandiose supports of self-esteem may be utilized.

Table 2.1 (cont.)

Level	Description
	Concern for the wellbeing of others may be considered less important than using others as tools for self-enhancement. Surprising shifts from vigor and boldness to states of apathy, boredom, or unpleasant restlessness may occur. Because of insufficient self-organization, the person may shift between being loving, then becoming suddenly overly demanding, and then becoming suddenly self-abasing and appeasing. Emotional governance is reduced. Undermodulated rage may erupt at others who are perceived as insulting and those are defensively blamed to avoid otherwise shameful deflations in the patient's self-esteem.
Disturbed	Life appears organized by using various self-states and some of them seem like a break with reality. Errors in self-other attribution occur. Undesirable self-attributes and emotions are projected from self to other. The actions of self and other may be confused in memory in terms of who did or felt what, and shifts in self-state may be accompanied by apparent forgetting of what happened in the alternative state of mind. Memories frequently combine fantasies with once real elements. State transitions can be explosive. Dissociative identity experiences reoccur under stress. Forgetting and then remembering may occur in segregated states of mind.
Fragmented	A massive chaos of selfhood can occur and, as a counter to cope with the high distress, the person frequently feels aroused to high defensiveness and accusation of others, as if under attack. As a needed repair of damage to self, the individual may regard self as merged with another person. Or, the person may withdraw in a hibernated, frozen, self-protecting coping effort that to others appears bizarre and self-damaging. Parts of the bodily self may be infused with the "badness" and the rest of the body may react to disown that part. This sense of chaos is very painful and can give rise to poorly regulated emotional impulses, including potentially suicidal or homicidal urges, often intensified further because the strange behaviors lead to social stigmatization.

The lower levels summarized in Table 2.1 involve maladaptive shifting of self-states and can lead to a chaotic sense of identity or extreme depersonalization and derealization (Bender, Morey, and Skodol, 2011). Skodol and colleagues (2011) and Zimmerman et al. (2012) suggest that clinicians use categories of identity, self-direction, empathy, and intimacy to observe and formulate levels of personality functioning, as exemplified in the work on Organizational Levels of Self and Other Schematization (Horowitz et al., 1984; Horowitz, 1991, 2014). The Psychodynamic Diagnostic Manual (Lingiardi et al., 2nd edition in 2016) defines this as the P-axis of personality functioning. The Diagnostic and Statistical Manual (5th edition, 2013) defines this in section III as levels of personality functioning.

In most psychotherapy, learning occurs in the context of a verbal conversational sequence embodied in a non-verbal sense of an adequate therapeutic alliance (Christian et al., 2012; Krupnick, 2012). The patient operating at a higher level of self-organization will see the therapist's intent and thereby learn this framework quickly and accurately. They show progress by using these skills to achieve a new level of authenticity in their relationships (Curtis, 2012).

Patients operating at lower levels of self-organization find it harder to process complex remarks made by the therapist. They have difficulty following the therapist's suggestions that clarify the patterns and origins of their current attitudes. If the therapist asks the patient to compare and contrast different views of a situation, the patient may become confused about the therapist's statements, questions, and intentions. In this case, it may help to ask the patient to repeat therapist's remarks to ensure understanding. A patient may report only part, or a distortion of parts of the therapist's remarks. If so, simpler and repeated comments may be necessary.

Self-other formulation

A patient's self-schemas, and well as the degree of coherence in their current self-organization, can be clarified by investigating their beliefs about the self that vary in different models of relationship scenarios (Stern, 1985, 2004; Kohut, 1972). A self-other model may represent *desired* transactions (which can manifest positive transference feelings), while another role-relationship model may represent *feared* transactions (which can manifest negative transference feelings). Other role-relationship models may represent a defense against dangerous emotions. These may have a *compromise* positioning of self to avoid acting on desires that could lead to dreadful consequences. An example of a compromise role-relationship model could be longing for a loving relationship while fearing the other's humiliating rejection, so therefore taking a defensive attitude of indifference to the other's feelings towards the patient.

The compromise protects from a wish-fear dilemma, but may reduce quality of life. This therapist should base formulations on a configuration of wish-fear-defense elements, some of which are not fully conscious. This formulation leans towards a future in which enhanced self-organization leads to less fear and less compromise, as well as more motivation for happiness.

Self-criticism is an important feature of the formulation of recurrent patterns. Multiple inner critics may coexist in a patient. Inner critics are part of self-organization that may also be experienced as spiritual figures, ancestors, or voices of parents. This highlights the importance of cultural considerations in case formulation since culture in its many forms influences the way patients make recurrent self-judgments. Harsh and conflicting patterns of self-judgement can become topics for attention in therapy.

Indeed, this complex matter is, in effect, a relationship of self with self, often a critic-self making value judgments about an expressing-self (Benjamin, 1979,

1987, 1996, 2003; Luborsky, 1984; Horowitz, 2005, 2011, 2014). In other words, a patient's level of self-organization is also observed and formulated in terms of how the patient feels, thinks, and behaves toward him- or herself. Are there negative biases in their attention to self? Is the patient self-rewarding or self-punishing? Self-judgmental attitudes are usually clarified when therapists ask patients for self-appraisals, such as a patient expressing "I am a failure." These attitudes form a part of prevailing negative biases in information processing, and part of degrading self-schemas.

Development of self-organization

A clinician's formulations can involve the foundations of identity begun in infancy and childhood, informed by a developmental framework of how self-concepts may have evolved in childhood. The effects of *attachment* and memories of adverse events are especially relevant (Bowlby, 1969; Kernberg, 1976; Horowitz, 2011, 2014; Beebe and Lachman, 2013; Frijda, 1986; Scherer, 1988; Smith & Lazarus, 1993; Sroufe, 1996; Horowitz, 1998). From an early fusion with the main parenting figure, a child forms a very basic self-schema (Pine, 1985; Stern, 1998; Beebe and Lachman, 2013).

Although normally developing babies can verbally refer to themselves and others by fifteen to eighteen months of age, much happens before these socially recognized self-and-other narrations. Normal infants will mimic an adult sticking out his or her tongue (Meltzoff, 2007, and Field, 2007 cited in Music 2011). Early relationships teach an infant how their actions are taken by others, and these codifications begin to organize emotional controls of the self.

Other people become differentiated as having different potential effects on self and safety. Stranger anxiety, which infants may exhibit at seven to ten months of age, illustrates the formation of attachment models. If an unknown person appears, especially when the baby is not being held in the arms of the caregiver, the baby may show a startled response by staring, exhibiting a fearful facial expression, or crying. The child may also turn to look at the face of a familiar figure, as if looking for emotional cues about how to respond to a stranger. If the parent seems calm, the child's threat response typically diminishes. If the parent routinely exhibits tension in reaction to these situations, the fear of strangers can endure. Temperament may dictate how easily a particular child is frightened and how quickly equilibrium can be recovered.

It seems to child development investigators that children, between two and four years of age, of parents who have provided relatively consistent care and nurturance acquire a soothing internal representation that begins to make the separation anxiety from the source of comfort and protection tolerable. These children view their parents as a secure base (Bowlby, 1969) from which to explore their world and to which they can return for replenishment. At this point, however, the experience is a new one, and separations that entail the child not being able to locate the caregiver may incite distress. So also will parental inconsistency such as a father who cares for a daughter and then in an alternate state of mind abuses her sexually.

A child's response to reconnection after separation may vary. Some children will ignore their mother's return after separation, some will remain distressed, some will be soothed, and some will display an uncoordinated, disorganized response (Ainsworth, 1978; Hesse & Main, 2000). These *attachment styles*, labeled *avoidant, ambivalent/resistant, secure,* and *disorganized/disoriented,* reflect the degree of safety and trust infants have formed in fundamental role-relationship schemas of the self with attachment figures (Ainsworth, 1978). Notably, research shows that infant attachment categories predict future emotional tendencies and adult self-regulatory capacities (Bowlby, 1989; Fonagy & Bateman, 2005; Main, 1975; Sroufe, 1979; Stayton & Ainsworth, 1973).

Although "good-enough" parenting (Winnicott, 1965) is not a monolithic category of behaviors, it seems to involve a parent's ability to reflect empathetically on children's internal self-experience and to act accordingly. This empathy reflects the child back to itself, giving information about self. Grienenberger, Kelly, and Slade's (2005) research supports this observation and speaks to the role that parental reflective functioning plays in a child's development of identity. Mothers with more advanced ability to understand their children's minds were more likely to have secure, attached children.

Conversely, mothers low in reflective functioning were more likely to have children with insecure attachment (disorganized or avoidant styles). Furthermore, mother-child affective communication—more specifically, mothers' response to their children's distress after separation—mediated the relationship between maternal behavior and child attachment. Results of such research suggest a link between attachment style, adult identity, and emotional regulation capacity (Fonagy, Steele, & Steele, 1991).

For some people, distress persists during later development during periods of separation from a person on whom they feel dependent. Derivatives of abandonment fears may be detected in a high frequency, intensity, and degree of emotional dysregulation that occurs with perceived threats of these separations (Milrod et al., 2014). In the stress of some impact on self-esteem, the person may experience an imperative need for support from another person. In desperation, even dangerous or exploitative relationships may be formed in order to avoid self-states of depersonalization or the terrifying emotional results of feeling chaotic and fragmented. Some dysfunctional marriages are sustained because the person anticipates, perhaps correctly, that they will become disorganized when reacting to the stress of a divorce. The death of a spouse may also lead to disorganization beyond a mourning response because of an additional loss of the self-maintaining function of the relationship.

If abandonment fears are formulated, a clinician can predict and prepare for problems that may arise when regular appointments are changed or the patient feels a need for more support. Formulation of a patient's attachment style can aid a therapist in understanding such behaviors as excessively calling the therapist between sessions or regressions in symptoms when the therapist is unavailable.

To recapitulate, formulations about developmental patterns can predict emotional regression. Adults with poor self-regulation may develop vulnerable self-schemas that foresee danger without a protective other. Distressed self-states may become more common in vulnerable patients when significant others (on whom they depend for a sense of security or wholeness) become unavailable because of death, divorce, emergency changes, or relationship ruptures.

Technique

Psychotherapy aims to clarify the recurring relationship problems and repetitive lapses in self-esteem that lead to problematic states of mind. Reasons for their development may be reconstructed. Insight into dysfunctional and distorted wishes, fears, and fantasies leads to growth through learning more rational attitudes. Clarifications and interpretations enhance the creation of new self-narratives.

The patient's capacity to reflect on multiple perspectives—their own as well as others'—aids this process and is itself progressively enhanced by new learning. Questions that enhance this learning often open a door within a topic, as in: "What do you think that person intended when he said xyz to you?" or "When you reconsider what he said, are you sure he meant to put you down rather than to suggest an alternative way for you both to do the activity?" Answers to such questions may increase insight and lead to discussion of rational alternative beliefs.

Goals for self are important to clarify and reprioritize. Many patients will be found to only vaguely connect their self-appraisals and their contributions in a realistic manner. Some have given up prematurely and others are too bold in expectations. The therapist brings attention to realistic possibilities and plans. The particular patient is encouraged to think about and reappraise connections between self-attributes, such as temperament and talent, and plans for taking steps to develop the skills and capacities needed to achieve desired social success and overcome feared consequences of trying to achieve goals.

The therapist may help clarify fantasies, such as becoming a rock star, honored parent, or great leader, to achieve greater understanding of self. Reappraisals are encouraged and the real-life steps necessary to achieve aspects, derivatives, or alternatives to these fantasies are considered. How would a good singing voice be trained? How would a good teacher be engaged? What degree of ambition might be attainable? How can values within self be harmonized by readjustments? These issues involve emotions ranging from pride to shame, and the potential for the latter must be safely contained in therapy before the ideas can proceed towards mastery and self-actualization. Attention focusing is gradually advanced.

The therapist views an intervention as an experiment. The reactions of the patient are the results. Were the actions helpful or not? The therapist may assess whether the patient understood (1) what was said by the therapist, and (2) why the therapist made the statement. When misunderstanding occurs, the therapist may formulate why. The patient's levels of function matter greatly in such formulations.

Imagine a patient functioning at a relatively high level of self-organization. At the higher levels of processing information, that patient may understand the therapist as saying:

"How are you feeling?" and then construct an appraisal such as:
"The therapist asks how am I feeling; thus I ask myself, how am I feeling? Hmm . . ." We can paraphrase this as, "the therapist intends to learn to experience me as I am experiencing within me. The therapist is joining with me for a shared view on what I may now say."

In contrast, a patient functioning at a lower level of self-organization may hear the word sequence:

"How are you feeling?" as if the therapist's intention were to embarrass, as if the paraphrase was the therapist saying:
"I just bet, you don't know how you are feeling, do you, you fool?"

Patients at lower levels of personality functioning are more likely to misinterpret what the therapist says as well as what the therapist intends by the remarks that were just made (Bateman and Fonagy, 2004; Luyten and Blatt, 2013). A patient experiencing a therapist as being mean, accusatory, or degrading can get angry. The hostility response to feeling attacked can be impulsively expressed. Hopefully, the patient can process the reaction and put it into words. That allows a conversational revision of the transference feelings and underlying attitudes.

Dealing with transference feelings

A patient with habitual separation anxiety may fear anger that might be activated in transference reactions. The reasons can be twofold. One, the anger could outrage the therapist and lead to their withdrawal or, two, the therapist might be harmed by the degree of the patient's outrage that inner emptiness is not being filled by the therapist. This transference phenomenon can result from a propensity for *misappraisals* of the actual frame in which the therapist operates (Fonagy & Target, 2000).

It is important for therapists to realize that a patient may experience *both* trust *and* an expectation of betrayal—one in which the therapist serves only his or her own interests and not the patient's best interest. This is an example of parallel processing, probably pre-consciously, of contradictory beliefs about the same person. The therapist may remark on the differences in attitude between the frame and the patient's transference feelings: but that is not likely to be understood if the patient is too flooded and too disorganized in the moment of the therapist's statements.

Emotions may intensify as the patient continues therapy, focusing on the attitudes that lead into a long-standing potential for deep feelings. The patient observes how the therapist reacts to expressions of emotion, in essence testing for safety and containment. The therapist shows non-verbally that he or she remains calm and non-judgmental. This calm state can increase the patient's ability to go further in examining otherwise threatening attitudes.

Clarification of patterns requires some self-reflective capacities. A patient with lifelong disturbances in self-schemas can slowly learn self-reflection and self-esteem from a new experience of trust, consistency, and acceptance as may be found in a gradually evolving understanding of the roles in a therapeutic alliance (Piper and Duncan, 1999; Levy et al, 2006; Shahar et al, 2010; Purcell, 2011; Morey et al., 2011). Therapy techniques useful at promoting improvements in patients at higher levels of personality functioning may not be helpful to those patients who operate at lower levels, and *vice versa* (Horowitz, Marmar, Weiss et al., 1984; Piper, Azim et al., 1991; Millon, 1999; Blatt et al., 1996; Høgland et al., 2006; Hamachi et al., 2009; Diener and Monroe, 2011; Mullin and Hilsenbroth, 2012). In general, simpler packages of clarification are necessary in patients currently functioning at lower levels of self-organization. Repetition is needed and learning takes longer.

Enhancing connectivity

One of the most important goals is to lessen dissociations between self-concepts, which will lead to experiences of more complex connections. Smoothing the transitions between states may be observed. If so, this allows the person to present a poised appearance in social situations, thereby improving chances for sustained respect and interaction.

When a patient is functioning at lower levels of self-integration, basic feelings may be experienced consciously as relatively sensorimotor representations with impoverished verbal representations. This should not be surprising because people develop many of their past concepts of identity and relationship to the world at the pre-verbal stages of development (McWilliams, 2011). The therapeutic process can help the patient represent these ideas clearly, using words, perhaps for the first time. Verbal statements aid in attitude modification.

In the context of therapy, the patient may recognize beliefs that seem inappropriate to the present, and work rationally, more rationally than usual, to clarify alternatives. The articulation of implicit ideas builds the conceptual skill of self-reflection, scaffolds the skill of empathy, and provides an opportunity to practice tolerance for difficult self-focused emotions such as self-disgust. When the patient notes the therapist's repetition of a specific clarification, he or she may be told that this is the therapist's intention, to enable new learning.

Some expressions will begin non-verbally, and the therapist's work of verbal clarification may enable the patient to learn how to verbalize feelings and attitudes. That will improve their ability to negotiate difficult situations with others, which in turn is likely to enhance self-esteem. When progress is taking place, some patients may be unaware that this is so, focusing as they do on current problems and states of distress. Saying what progress has occurred helps increase morale and reflection. For example, a clinician can tell a patient that when therapy started, it was hard for him to put his feelings into words, and now he is able to do so to a greater and more useful extent.

Summary

Personality growth occurs as a result of the integration of elements within unconscious cognitive maps of self-organization. It includes restructuring of complex meanings and ways of processing information. Levels of present integration may be inferred from the shared observations of the therapist and the patient. The ongoing process of formulation determines the therapist's prediction of the likely effect of a given therapeutic intervention on the patient. Patients at a lower level of functioning generally require more supportive interventions, including answering questions, giving advice, and providing repeated signs of compassionate care. Complex linking of interpretations may not be more confusing than helpful. At higher levels of functioning, in order to promote progress, therapists can utilize more complex pattern clarifications, interpretations, reconstructions of development of maladaptive beliefs, and challenges to avoidance behaviors.

3

Identity functioning and self-states

Patients have levels of social functioning that range from a highly coherent identity to fragmented self-organization. One disturbance in identity functioning discussed in the last chapter was the difference between smooth and explosive transitions in self-presentation (Horowitz, 2013, 2014; Wachtel, 2014). In this chapter, we go deeper into observations of emotional control during therapy sessions and how to formulate these observations to influence technique. These formulations attempt to address the question of why a patient may enter states in which the self feels powerless over its ideas and feelings.

Observing transitions from one state to another

A patient may be discussing distress from feeling potentially resentful and enraged by certain social conditions. The therapist aims to detect a change from well-modulated to poorly controlled expressions of anger. The patient may seem to verge on under-modulation of emotional intensity, followed by reducing their distress by putting up shields that conceal any possible expression of irritation. The patient might then stay in an over-controlled state with flat affect for a certain period. These are examples of well-modulated, under-modulated, and over-modulated states discussed in this chapter.

Transitions between states of mind are key observations. Consider a case in which a patient has been calmly recounting recent outside events. She then shifts into a state of belligerence toward the therapist, accusing him of not being helpful enough. The therapist is challenged to come up with a solution for the patient. The patient is also checking to see how the therapist handles a threat to his self-esteem (e.g., "You are so incompetent, Dr. Psychobabble"). The patient's aggression may cause the therapist to react with heightened vigilance. Of note, observing changes in the therapist's self-state are as important as observing the patient's shifts.

Gut-level sensations are key to the therapist's self-observations. Suppose a patient becomes hostile and the therapist observes their own shift into a state of hyper-alertness. Being familiar with such instances, the therapist remains quiet and calm. The patient may intensify expressions of hostility; perhaps even seem to be close to losing control. The therapist wants to observe what happens next, focusing on certain questions. Can the patient now move away from an *under-modulated state* of angry attacking and enter into and stabilize a *well-modulated state* of competent self-reflection? Will the patient appear to disguise their irritation by assuming an air of careful and guarded politeness, identifiable as an *over-controlled state*?

For example, a patient named Henry was having problems with his business partner. He needed his partner's financial advice but found dealing with him prickly and unpleasant. In therapy, Henry described the way he managed the conflict and expressed his own feelings of frustration. As he did so, his emotions, while complex, became clearer to both himself and the therapist. These complex emotions went beyond simple anger. His verbal and non-verbal expressive manner signaled that he knew the therapist was listening and understanding his feelings. He used reflective self-awareness within a protective emotional container, exhibiting a well-modulated state. He was working safely on a topic of importance within the framework of a therapy team.

Let us examine how Henry's well-modulated states differed from his over- and under-modulated ones.

Well-modulated states

In a well-modulated state, a patient exhibits good self-management. Even on distressing topics, the spoken words and accompanying non-verbal expressions usually seem harmonious. In this example, Henry could feel and express negative feelings without having to stop the flow of his expressions.

Over-modulated states

In therapy sessions, the therapist observed that Henry occasionally shifted out of a well-modulated state and entered into an over-modulated state. Henry seemed to erect a shield of self-concealment, a shift in expressive style. In this state he avoided eye contact, chose his words too carefully, and seemed to veil the facial movements of his eyes and mouth. The therapist first noted this shift to an over-modulated state when Henry began to discuss the topic of frustrations with his wife. On that topic, his speech took on a muted quality and he talked in bland generalities instead of addressing specifics.

Under-modulated states

In an under-modulated state, a person's usual degree of self-governance appears diminished. Henry, who had just been so guarded when discussing his relationship with his wife, suddenly shifted from an over-modulated to an under-modulated state of mind. He let go of a burst of emotional statements about how his wife had embarrassed him in front of his friends the night before, making him feel a mixture of rage and shame. While recounting the story, he raised his voice; he clenched his fists, his mouth tightened, and his eyes glared while looking wildly around the room.

In response, the therapist began to speak slowly, summarizing what had happened in the last few minutes. The therapist continued to repeat factual statements rather than ask questions. In time, Henry calmed down. The session could then continue in a more controlled emotional state.

Shimmering states

There are gradations and oscillations between well-modulated, under-controlled, and over-controlled states. At times, especially in well-modulated states when a patient is trying to express deeper emotions (as when Henry began to talk about his marital feelings and/or when a person wants to reduce emotional intensity), there may be a "shimmering" quality—an oscillation between expressive and avoidance maneuvers.

A *shimmering state* contains antithetical elements, and may include both over- and under-modulated aspects. It is the discord in visible signs that indicate that the patient is struggling to express a conflict while avoiding some of their associated feelings. Noting the shimmering state leads to useful formulations and techniques. Characteristics can include uneven emotional inflections in voice, halting speech, wandering attention, the relaying of incomplete ideas, a tendency to shy away from or retract already expressed ideas, a vaguely jittery feeling, or the rapid reversal of beliefs or values.

Henry, who seemed so impulsively hostile toward his wife in an under-modulated state, told the therapist while he was in an over-modulated state that he felt he had become used to their disagreements and did not need to discuss them further. The therapist then said, "You don't have to discuss that if it doesn't seem safe enough to do so, even here with me." While saying this, the therapist appeared non-judgmental and yet was implicitly suggesting continuing the topic. This was when Henry shifted into a shimmering state: his eyes filled with tears and his fingers nervously plucked at the stitches on the arms of the office chair he was seated in. He also spoke very haltingly. Now in this state, he talked about marital disagreements, including who said what to whom, and with what emotional reactions.

Formulation

Patients often want to reduce the threat of entering a dreaded, under-modulated state of mind. Formulation is enhanced as the clinician observes what topics lead into dreaded or undesirable self-states, and what defensive processes are used to avoid them. These are important topics to address in the increasingly safe conversations between patient and therapist.

Now one can begin to formulate the reasons for state transitions. A patient who has been operating from a certain understanding of the existing therapeutic alliance may shift to some other state, perhaps to one in which transference feelings emerge intensely. They could potentially move to a state of mind in which he or she confuses the therapist's remarks as manipulations rather than attempts to help clarify what is occurring.

The patient may also shift into a highly threatened self-state in which they regard the clinician as a predator, thus having a confused array of emotions, including fear and anger. This state may also shift explosively to one in which the patient wants to hurt him or herself because he or she may sense they have acted inappropriately. This last example could be considered a *state and relationship cycle*.

The pattern of a cycle may begin with a willing exploration, but then the patient may suddenly experience this exploration of their emotionality as dangerous and feel threatened by the therapist. Lastly, in a third phase of the cycle, the quality of badness is viewed within the patient's own self, and shame and shame-avoidance defenses become prominent.

A cycle of states may contain different self-presentations that are based on different self-schemas. Each self-presentation may seem to express a different quality, motive, or value about goals. The various self-schemas each comprise a configuration of attitudes. In this configuration, the therapist can formulate the dynamics of struggles between wishes, fears, and compromises intended to rescue the patient from a moral dilemma, such as acting towards gratifying a desire. Inner motives, including unconscious aims, often involve dilemmas: the *desire* contrasts with the *threat* of displeasure or harm to self or others, which can happen if desires are acted upon without regard to basic values. Sometimes a cycle of state transitions enacts aspects of a configuration of role-relationship models that endures in the patient's mind as a wish-fear dilemma. The patient may unconsciously hold a compromise model with scenarios that are self-protective but not self-actualizing. The overall formulation is a wish-fear-defense psychodynamic configuration.

Consider a patient who has both a dependent sense of self and a desire to be attached to someone who will provide nurture, care, and guidance. Separation anxiety may have been a developmental problem, as discussed in Chapter 2. As part of this wish, there may be *self and other scenarios* that, in effect, ask for the empathy and love or compassion from a "needed" other.

However, the dependent person may also have dreaded scenarios, such as anticipating that if he or she expressed the wish for care, the other might reject such an expression as too demanding, weak, or needy. The rejection is the fear. The self conceptualization in this scenario may have attributes of being both too needy and too complaining. When active, such a self-schema can lead to fear of being seen by others as having such traits. The person may have an abiding vulnerability to feeling shame from past devaluation experiences such as rejection and harsh criticism from authority or parental figures.

The dependent person in the example above has a set of unconscious expectations that include this *wish-fear dilemma*. If he seeks care, he may get what he wants, but he may also get what he fears. Here, the person may be experiencing *a state cycle* of supplication, satisfaction, rejection, and self-loathing. This unconscious expectation may take time to clarify and alter in therapy because the concepts have previously been largely pre-verbal.

The *configuration of scenarios* often have a protective component. In a *compromise self-schema*, the self might be conceptualized as self-sufficient or presented to others as such. This self-sufficiency could indicate increased capacity for autonomy, or it may be only a posture and inwardly feel like a *false self*.

The goal here is to learn how to configure self-schemas harmoniously. This means gradually reorganizing these varied self-schemas into a supraordinate self-schema. This would be learned through new experiences and in becoming able to feel a new identity as an autonomous person who is also able to regard the self in rich, interdependent relations with others.

Technique

The formulations just discussed allow a therapist to infer a patient's tangle of motives: certain wishful intentions of the patient as well as his or her fearful expectations and avoidance maneuvers. Yet, patients may not have learned to verbally express their intentions. What lies behind customary action patterns may remain unarticulated, inaccessible to conscious reflection or consideration. The therapist uses a number of techniques to help the patient put intentions and related expectations into words.

The therapist begins with clarifications to show patterns as *cause and effect scenarios*. As the patient reports a story from his or her life, the therapist asks for connections as well as the patient's interpretation of the event and its possible meanings. The goal is to clarify and modify layers of the patient's *dysfunctional beliefs*. Techniques for moving towards that goal vary with formulation of the patient's current level of integration, as discussed in Chapter 2.

At lower levels of self-organization, as shown in Table 2.1, a person may be impaired in self-control, self-direction, or self-presentation. When shifts in self-states occur, emotional expressions may appear explosive, and the patient may be regarded as unpredictable or threatening by others in social situations, including the therapist if countertransference feelings occur. For that reason, it is harder to deploy techniques of clarification, and slow repetitions of simple phrases are often necessary.

Explosive changes in a cycle of states will make most therapists feel uncomfortable, and some may feel an urge to "do something." The therapist might wish to say something like, "You seem to repeat a pattern with me that is directed at your father, as you told me last week. And then you start feeling worthless and having suicidal thoughts." Yet, this attempted clarification and interpretation is unlikely to soothe the patient or place him into a calmer state of mind. Interpretation of what is happening may in that moment be beyond the patient's information-processing capacity.

Such a patient may in the present moment be functioning at a disturbed level of cognitive processing; he or she may not be able to compare and contrast the different phrases spoken by the therapist. The implicit meaning—"You are angry at me because . . ."—is not comprehended by the patient as a point of comparison with how the patient felt toward his or her father. Additionally, the suggestion of a connection between an episode of hostility and the ensuing suicidal thoughts may also not be clear to the patient. The patient may feel again as if attacked by the therapist! In summary, the patient's conscious and self-reflecting mind is in this state unable to recognize the pieces of the cycle the therapist is attempting to clarify.

In such situations, it is important for the therapist to appear calm. Such calm responses and empathic soothing may help the patient deactivate transference schemas and reinstate the therapeutic alliance. If so, some progress may be gained by clarifying what is happening in a way that increases the patient's ability to reactivate a more competent set of self-concepts and realistic appraisal of what the therapist is intending.

For example, the therapist might say something like, "You were telling me about the criticism leveled at your work by your supervisor, and then we found our conversation to get somewhat perturbed. I think you may be feeling a bit unsettled right now. Would you like me to open the window for some fresh air? If we take a moment to breathe maybe we can try to find our rhythm again." The patient listening to the therapist may not process any of the ideas, but the therapist's demeanor and flowing words may reinstate a schema of being safe together.

The therapist must then decide whether or not to make the more complex remarks that might be spoken to a higher-functioning patient. This would depend on inferences about the patient's information-processing capacities in that particular moment.

There are two main points to understand regarding handling patients with currently highly disturbed levels of personality functioning. The first is that what the patient understands in one state may not be available to the patient's working memory in another state, even if the state shift occurs within minutes during the same therapy session. Due to *dissociative processes*, what is perceived in an early part of a cycle of states may not be remembered later. The second point is that once a well-modulated state has been reinstalled, short and simple clarifications by the therapist may be understood by the patient, but longer and more complex interpretations may not be well processed.

Techniques to enhance safe emotional expression

In therapy for personality growth, a person can learn richer and more flexible ranges of expression. For example, Jim, an intelligent 35-year-old business executive, displayed a limited range of emotional expression, and habitually seemed to over-control his emotions. He complained about a complete lack of joy in both his work and his social life. He also spoke of his general withdrawal from the world and his use of alcohol as a sedative.

Jim was concerned about the security of his job. He had allowed himself to accumulate significant credit card debt, and he could not afford to be out of work. He worried that he would soon be fired, which, when he described the situation in transactional detail, seemed like a real possibility. Worry was a thought process he labeled, but he could not elaborate on other self-conceptual and emotional qualities within his frequent worried states of mind.

With questions about cause and effect sequences, Jim pinpointed the start of his downward spiral at work as the period immediately following his promotion. He had developed an innovative approach to market his company's products and had been rewarded with a raise and increased responsibility. Jim's new duties included supervising a small staff and delivering periodic reports on the progress of his unit to management. These were highly stressful tasks.

The therapist asked for details and often used the traditional question: "And how did that make you feel?" Sometimes the therapist supplied words that might fit, such as vexed, irritated, frustrated, tense, angry, or frightened. In response, Jim learned to say more. He stated that he would get frustrated and then withdraw when the people he supervised did not meet his expectations. He felt frightened and embarrassed when he was being criticized by his manager.

Jim and the therapist soon agreed that it would be useful for him to be able to pay attention to the pattern of withdrawal he used to avoid potentially emotionally charged states. Avoidance was a way of coping: he felt he would fail at work if hostility emerged and if he harassed his staff. The therapist and he discussed that there were possible alternative maneuvers in between withdrawing from staff contact and venting at them. The alternatives were gradually examined through role-playing scenarios in therapy. This allowed Jim to try new strategies at work.

Progressively, Jim felt more in control of what he might say verbally to people with whom he was frustrated by keeping his non-verbal self-presentation calm. He noticed when there were situations of calm cooperation with his team.

Jim accepted the clarification that withdrawal was a defense against revealing what might be hostility. Together, he and the therapist drew up a list of the various reasons he felt frustrated by the actions of his staff. Jim was also afraid of a state he had seen in his father, a blind self-destructive rage. Seeing this aspect in his own developmental history helped him understand that he had learned to be over-controlled in order to avoid flying into the same blind rage as his father. He feared crushing others if he had strong, aggressive impulses. Inversely, he feared that they could crush him by bad evaluations of his performance as their manager.

On entry to a therapy session, to which the therapist was a few minutes late, Jim muttered to himself: "Typical tardy doctor. He couldn't care less about me!" However, he quickly retracted his statement when he realized the therapist had heard it, and apologized by stating: "Sorry, just kidding." The therapist used this series of remarks as a learning opportunity—a here-and-now situation that would be useful to look at.

The therapist told Jim that the feeling seemed to be irritation, and that Jim's criticism of the therapist suggested a belief that he did not care about Jim's treatment session or his progress. Jim struggled to express his feelings, but began by using some of the words the therapist supplied. Gradually, he began to use his own words. Through this process, Jim developed a state of anger that he could modulate successfully. In the privacy of his mind, he called this state *appropriate irritation*.

Later, Jim applied some new tactics at work. In some instances of mild annoyance, such as when a colleague had misspelled his name, he had a direct and moderate response. Here, his potential for excessive criticism and sharpness remained reasonably restrained. He controlled his face, voice, and posture as he asserted himself appropriately, spoke to the issue, maintained respect for the person he was confronting, and smoothly moved past the inciting topic. The self-image he learned through repetition during such states felt more competent.

Jim had an additional state of anger that appeared over-modulated. As the therapist drew attention to those qualities as a recurrent pattern, Jim named this state his *sullen, grudging state.* This followed earlier work, in which the therapist had encouraged him to develop some names for his recurrent states. In this sullen, grudging state, he shut down, backed off, and pouted. For example, when he was denied a position on a committee during a meeting, he became withdrawn and silent for the rest of that meeting. He initially believed his impassiveness protected him. In time, however, he came to realize that others could read beneath his mask.

When in his sullen, grudging state within a therapy session he spoke in a slow, surly, monotone voice. His self-concepts during this state included self-images as needy, aggrieved, and under-nurtured. Soon, however, with focused work, he could recognize his entry into this state, and also find his own way out of it. Jim was a bright man. On an intellectual level, he certainly understood that emotions cannot be expunged from his experience, but he needed to develop a much deeper understanding of how unconscious attitudes have an inner psychological reality beyond logic or rational thought.

Soon, Jim realized that harsh self-judgments were part of his underlying concern and an important theme to examine. This led the discussions in therapy to examine how and why critical attitudes had developed. What emerged was that Jim had a *wish-fear dilemma*: he wanted the excitement and pleasure associated with presenting his creative ideas, yet presenting them left him scared of falling embarrassingly short of some perfectionistic standard.

Jim's dilemma created anxious anticipation, which often led him to defensively withdraw into his office and enter a state that he and the therapist named *ruminative rehearsal.* In this state of mind, organized by the self-concept of being a creative person, Jim would repeatedly go over what he would show his colleagues in advance of a presentation, all the while continuing to maintain the feeling of not being ready to present his ideas publicly. Although checking his plans many times gave him reassurance that he was reducing the potential for embarrassment, this compulsive repetition also contributed to excessive procras-tination, creating more discomfort and anxiety, ultimately leading to greater potential embarrassment.

Labeling states like *ruminative rehearsal* helped Jim use his growing skill of *reflective conscious awareness* to combat habitual traits of both perfectionism and procrastination. He began to see unhealthy patterns, which he would then try to modify. He gradually learned to move forward without procrastination and to negotiate with others in a more satisfactory and controlled way. He could express his feelings when appropriate and in moderation.

Jim had a complex configuration of multiple self-schemas, operating largely outside of awareness. By examining those beliefs that could be verbalized, he was able to acknowledge his behavior and hence able to gradually modify them. Jim was formulated as having large discrepancies between a *realistic* self-schema, and an *ideal* self-schema of what the self should be. He also had *degraded* self-schema where he saw himself as a failure.

Jim's *ideal* self might feel admirable for his brilliant and unique contributions to society. His *degraded* self might feel that his self should suffer for not accomplishing his goals. Through the therapy, Jim's *realistic* self-schema evolved with the concept that trying to do one's best justifies and deserves pride.

Summary

Once clear patterns are formulated, both the patient and therapist can begin to understand the reasons behind the patient leaving a well-modulated state to enter into either an under- or over-modulated state. As shared understanding grows, by naming states and observing potential impending state transitions, a patient can begin to anticipate them. This adds a small but valuable feeling of improvement to their sense of emotional self-control. The patient may learn to act before a shift into an under-modulated state, deploying attention in a way that can stabilize their well-modulated state, either by focusing on ways to contemplate ideas in a slowed down and more reasoned manner or taking a time-out from the topic. The patient learns that conscious coping can replace unconscious defenses.

4

Possibilities for change in self-narratives

Self-narratives are continuous stories about the self that span the past, present, and future. Patients tell therapists their stories, and this evolving self-narrative becomes their life story. Understanding and unity across the time frames (past, present, and future) can produce more harmony in self-organization and reduce identity discord. The therapist helps the patient progress towards coherence by dealing in depth with topics of concern.

How can therapy develop self-narratives? Interacting with the patient's motives for treatment, the therapist creates a safe environment by deepening a therapeutic alliance. The patient feels protected from the more extreme moods that revelations might produce. Then, gradually, the patient and therapist talk about irrational beliefs and possible deficiencies in social appraisals. Together they seek new solutions to the patient's unresolved problems. Both therapist and patient share the goals of examining outmoded self-concepts and advancing the continuity of identity coherence.

Observing states of mind indicates topics of concern. Formulation of the meanings in these topics clarifies maladaptive beliefs about the self and also leads to inferences about how attitudes first developed as early stories about what happened in childhood. Currently dysfunctional attitudes may have had a useful function when they were formed. Understanding the difference between a child's rudimentary efforts to cope and an adult's enhanced abilities is part of advancing self-narratives. Formulations increase understanding and lead to techniques for helping the patient modify limiting attitudes (Lodi-Smith et al., 2009; McLean and Fournier, 2008)

Observation

The topics addressed in therapy are usually brought up directly or indirectly by the patient in the opening minutes of the session. Sometimes the therapist begins the process by asking what happened in an anticipated event or inquiring about some kind of homework. Together, the patient and the therapist may then jointly choose where to focus. The therapist is alert to signs of an important topic that involves dysfunctional or conflicting beliefs.

Avoidance or lapses in emotional regulation may be signs that indicate a topic of concern. In the previous chapter we discussed shifts into over- and under-modulated states of mind. Sometimes a patient reports the unexpected, unbidden emergence of images, memories, or fantasies. This is another sign of incomplete topic processing.

For example, suppose the patient is exploring their personal meaning of a recent adverse event, such as a loss. As the story unfolds over several sessions, an element may emerge intrusively into conscious representation, such as a specific image or pang of feeling. The subtopic in the intrusive episode should be formulated and explored further.

Intrusive ideas and feelings are common when a patient is under life stress or working through memories of traumatic experiences. They can also arise from internal stress alone, such as an excessive emotional reaction to an ordinary occurrence. An example of that was discussed in Chapter 2: the patient reported feeling queasy and seemed anxious right after the therapist spoke of a necessary change in appointments. This shared observation allowed clarification of similar observations in the patient's life, such as when a friend canceled a planned meeting. Such patterns were repetitive but not yet understood.

Naming topics deserving more attention

Thus far, we have discussed finding self-narrative topics to address in therapy by 1) observing shifts in state, especially leaving a well-modulated state for a defensive or poorly-modulated one; and 2) observing intrusive ideas and feelings that emerge unbidden. Now we can add: 3) patient avoidance of topics that seem incomplete. As we will see, if a patient has a pattern of repeatedly switching away from a topic, it may indicate avoidance of emerging ideas and emotions. This prevents completion of trains of thought that can lead to new kinds of decision-making from reappraisals.

Sometimes it is easier to observe defensiveness than to observe the concepts and potential feelings that are present as an active conflict within a topic. The defensiveness may be a shift away when the patient's remarks so far have revealed only the tip of an iceberg. Just a few associations have peeked above the surface. Making the observation of a switch away from what was being expressed as a train of thought suggests paying more attention and taking a deeper look at what might lay beneath the surface. Naming a topic helps the therapist in implementing the intention to pay subsequent attention to possibly warded-off mental contents.

Take the example of separation anxiety related to the therapist's actions. The patient may be talking about how irritating it was that sessions were changed to accommodate some other function of the clinician. In the midst of that, before finishing this sentiment, the patient switches word choices and tone. The expression of irritation vaguely directed towards the therapist switches to conciliatory tonalities vaguely directed towards the therapist. The words selected by the patient are suddenly solicitous, sympathizing with the many demands and responsibilities that the patient is aware the therapist must have. The switching indicates a fear of directly expressing irritation. Potential irritation at becoming disconnected from the therapist is masked by the defense of pseudo-solicitousness.

A fourth observation in addition to state shifts, intrusions, and topic-switches concerns premature closure by making a sudden critical judgment. A topic is then regarded as if closed because blame for distress has been assigned. Blame has not been fully explored, but rather placed on the self (as in self-appraisals that seem automatic and harsh) or another person (as in the case of Silver in Chapter 1, who disrupted realistic analysis of cause-and-effect stories by prematurely and irrationally blaming others).

Formulation

Anna and self-disgust

Anna was observed to talk as if she were helplessly and hopelessly trapped in a pattern of self-subordination and reactive self-disgust. Anna agreed that this topic of self-subordination and inadequate assertiveness deserved repeated, safe, and slow exploration. She also wanted to avoid the topic of self as subordinate because it led towards hopelessness and self-loathing.

In one example, Anna felt disgusted with herself because she had worked overtime when it was not necessary. When asked to do so by her boss she reported that she had experienced a powerful sense of foreboding. To get away from a sense of impending doom when the request was made, she had agreed to work overtime even though doing so was quite inconvenient for her.

Her boss had asked her to stay after hours to finish a task that was not essential, and staying late interfered with her getting to a planned meeting with friends on time. She gave a few details of why she had agreed to stay at work in spite of the inconvenience. Before she acquiesced, she observed within herself an unpleasant dread of what she expected to happen if she said no, even if she were to have done so in an appropriately polite, and tactful way. Her intuition told her he would get angry.

Her thinking was not so clear about how she would have responded to his expression of anger if it had occurred. Formulation from other similar episodes helped the therapist and patient uncover what was going on in her mind in the preconscious expectations. She said the threat of his anger felt like her internal expectation and not anything she had reason to anticipate about this particular boss.

The therapist said, "Well let's imagine a kind of theater stage in your mind's eye. On it, a scene unfolds. Your boss asks an actress, representing you, to work overtime. She politely says she cannot this evening. Then what happens?" She shuddered at this very moment in therapy, entering a shimmering state of mind. She was shocked to realize that in the present moment she had the same feeling of impending doom. She said this was familiar, and when she felt like that she wanted to escape from the therapy office.

She did not want to say any more about an imagined scenario because she did not want her fear to become even more intense. With the therapist's support, however, she admitted that the "terrible" seemed more tolerable. Anna said she could go on.

Anna imagined that her boss would glare at her and stalk out silently. The therapist said, "Hmm . . ." (They sat silently together.) Then the therapist went on, "Well, I guess you have an expectation of a pretty major attack, the kind that can make you feel frail. Also, in your imagination, he would walk out on you. We've heard that theme before."

"Yes," said Anna. She remained in a shimmering, working state. She continued, "Like I have told you my mother got enraged and I felt demolished." Anna and the therapist were able to talk on, about how she anticipated a repetition of childhood traumatic experiences of corrosive maternal rage directed at her.

As she became capable of conscious reflection and expression, she was able to distance herself from the trauma memories and abandonment threats. She gained a more assertive realization of her adult qualities. Even with an angry boss, she now had enough personal strength not to fragment into identity chaos.

When she told the therapist of the traumatic memories of her mother's periodic and paranoid rages and her own terrible feelings of being doomed, Anna gradually realized how she had unconsciously applied a cognitive map of how she felt as a verbally assaulted child to a current situation in which she was not actually being assaulted. Cognitive maps are attitudes that can change. Once she could verbalize her fear of being "demolished," Anna could tell herself that she was too timid, and too frequently submissive, but her self-organization was not in great danger. She talked about learning and repeating more positive attitudes about herself.

In her rage attacks, Anna's mother told her she was born of a bad seed and that she had become a very bad child, and that no doubt Anna would become quite a bad adult eventually. Anna of course did feel bad as a result, and to some extent blamed herself for causing her mother's shift to rage. Losing her good mother and being assaulted by her bad mother led her to dissociate the views into good and bad self-states.

Anna could recall very little about what she was like at six years of age. Now as an adult she could use reflective thinking in conversation with the therapist to attempt to reconstruct what was probable in the past. She was probably not a terrible child. She probably did not deserve the accusations of bad character that her paranoid mother attributed to her. These formulations helped her make linkages of identity narratives from the past to the present, and Anna came to think of herself more coherently and with fewer dissociations.

People present themselves to others as they want to be seen and "identified" (Goffman, 1974). The ways people prefer to be viewed by others are often better than their critical internal views of themselves. Ann at first presented herself to the therapist as a well-behaved docile person. Then Anna oscillated ambivalently between good and bad self-states. The pattern in therapy was similar to the pattern at work.

She always tried to present herself to her boss as a compliant, nice woman, who would not be a cause of frustration to him. This felt incongruent with her actual feelings. She was not only afraid of her boss becoming angry; she sensed emergent anger at him in herself. She feared his reactive attack on her and her intensified attack on him. Passivity and compliance were the defenses built into the formation of her character. Anger frightened her and she stifled it. She felt vaguely inauthentic until her self-narrative improved and she could balance assertiveness with composure against her habitual submissive defenses.

Like Anna, some patients feel that they almost always present false self-images. Inwardly they may experience a sense of inauthenticity in these self-presentations. Winnicott (1989) theorized that a sense of an inward false self could result from highly disturbing relationship experiences in early childhood. Anna could not as a child realistically process her strong emotional reactions to the verbal abuse from her mother because her self-organization was still so immature. Such a child may have to resort to gross distractions, including diverting from direct external observations and internal sensations to fantasies and dissociative experiences.

A traumatized child might believe that the motives for the parental abuse are not to be questioned and as a result believe the pain and distress are deserved. She then may start developing self-concepts as bad in some way. She may then form an enduring sense that this image of self as bad is realistic, that the parenting figures believe it, and that she truly has enduring bad qualities inside her. A configuration of dissociated good and bad self-states can be schematized, interfering with the development of coherent self-organization.

As with Anna, dissociative experiencing of self-states can take place between a "good self" that deserves kindness and a "bad self" that deserves aggression from others. By self-identifying with the parental role of aggression, the child may also develop self-concepts as a bad, but strong aggressor. The child may learn both self-roles: as aggressor and as victim. Dyadic completion tendencies will cast others in the opposite role.

Childhood traumas are inscribed experiences in the mind/brain and can color adult patterns, which then are enacted without full conscious appreciation or choice. Consciously, Anna felt impending doom. The re-enactment scenarios were formed into schemas during her mother's rage states and these in the present were largely unconscious. The goal in therapy was to safely contain her emergent anger and frustrated love-yearning, utilizing the empathy of the therapist.

If safety could moderate her feelings to tolerable levels, without disrupting the therapeutic alliance, she and the therapist could have an ongoing reformulation of what happened in the past, what was happening in transference feelings, and what could happen in outside relationships. Capacities to help form this new self-narrative included reducing dissociative processes and enhancing reflective self-awareness.

This growth process involved two kinds of activities in Anna's mind. One was reprocessing her memories, reconsidering what it all meant now with new adult appraisals. The second change process involved learning from the new relational experience with the therapist. For Anna, that meant learning the safety of assertiveness and expressing to the therapist her yearning, frustration, and anger.

As in the case of Anna, childhood experiences of stress, strain, and trauma are hard to assimilate with sustained good and valuable self-concepts if during and after them, parental figures fail to offer a genuine reflection of the child's actual good nature. Understanding some developmental theory in this regard may enhance formulation of how childhood experiences may live on in the mind, as potential attitudes that are inappropriate to adult contexts, but nonetheless repeated in a way that seems compulsive.

Applying theory to possible formulations

Klein (1940, 1976) hypothesized that when a child experiences negative feelings, the mother figure may be blamed due to a primitive kind of externalization. Melanie Klein (1940) called this a *paranoid position*, an irrational role relationship model depicting others as the source of inner distress. A potential for anger arousals creates a negative emotional valence. In later child development, Klein believed the child advanced to self-blame for relational distress. In this *depressive position*, the child would believe what could be put later into words as, "I am to blame for all this distress. I do only wrong. The situation is so sad, but I do not know how to make the future any better." This kind of self-talk could lead to the triad of common adult depressive thoughts described by Beck (1976): "the future is hopeless, I am bad, and no one can help me." Cognitive scientists call this a negative attentional bias. The patient comes to believe that no future relationship is possible, that no identity strengthening can occur, and that no one can help. This leads to traits of vulnerability, negative emotional valence, and to a high potential to have feelings of emptiness, pessimism, and fear.

This theory suggests it is useful to consider the degree to which the continuity and constancy of secure attachments protected the growing self-organization of a child who has become an adult (Bowlby, 1989). Did abuse or neglect impair coherent development? Were there dissociative, uncorrected discords in self-structures of meaning? If so, there may be a need for a new self-narrative, mastering past traumas and attention to repetition of new attitudes that will lead towards expecting less victimization as an adult (Herman, 1997). On the other hand, parent-blaming stereotypes should be avoided in favor of individualized formulations.

Kohut (1972) took such formulations about early relationships a step further in considering difficulties in developing a strong and coherent self-organization because of the patient's paucity of experiences in empathic attunement. Kohut contrasted growth in self-coherence with an enfeebled sense of identity vulnerability. He identified a partial self–other fusion that could lead self to expect others as extensions of self rather than as independent agents with their own needs. He used the term self-object for this construct.

Interestingly, not only may a child use a parenting figure as a self-object, but the consistent caregiver may also use the child as a self-object. Both gain identity, satisfaction, and even pride from attachment to the other. Unfortunately, parental figures might have used the child as an extension of themselves, failing to empathically tune in to and reflect back the qualities of the emerging self within the child. As a result of the absence of true empathy and compassion, the child might emerge into adulthood vulnerable to identity disturbances and shame states (Winnicott, 1969; Ferro, 2011). When a therapist is aware of such possible etiologies of the formation of self-organization, he or she can improve formulations to help the patient gain insight into current patterns and build confidence in change by learning how to explore, test, and use better opportunities for relationship richness.

The unconscious attitudes of infancy and childhood lay down a structure that, if not modified during development, can lead to a variety of maladaptive self-states. These may lead an adult to make unrealistic self-judgments, especially under stress. A conscious sense of self-esteem and identity coherence can be disturbed by unconscious self-criticisms and unjustified attitudes. Formulation of these attitudes can lead to conceptualization of how to help a patient review stories of the past, as enacted in the present.

Technique

Observation can highlight and label topics that deserve further attention. Formulation leads to improved observations, formulations and techniques. The therapist shares some aspects of this process with the patient and gently guides attention to the themes that seem important, even if unclear. Patients usually agree intuitively that the topics the therapist observed and described are worthwhile to explore, even as they also resist doing so to avoid the unpleasant emotions that are connected to the topics.

Clarification of the pattern with the patient is the first step towards a shared formulation process. Setting goals for pattern modification comes next. New experiences in relation to the pattern itself occur with the therapist and can modify patterns such as habitual avoidance of expressing feelings. The patient is helped by the therapist to clarify his or her intention, enabling enhanced self-reflective awareness.

Enhanced review by the patient of what he or she just said is a sign of progress that may be shared with the patient. Leaning such capacities as reappraisal helps most patients in learning how to revise stories. In this way insight may be added to the new experiences of safety in frank communication of emotional issues and irrational beliefs. Insight is additive.

The therapist acts to promote insight, when indicated, by *interpreting* the reasons that certain dysfunctional attitudes may have developed. The therapist does not know for sure, and may be following general theory and intuition; thus it is prudent to share a cautious, experimental attitude with the patient. Techniques are experiments, leading to more observations, revised formulations, and better reconstructions and narratives.

Many attitudes that require interpretation are residues of childhood beliefs. These may include over-simplistic and unrealistic explanations of why the person felt consistently unloved. Self-narratives can mature so that extrapolations from the past are put into words, and thus modified by more adult versions of an ongoing life story. Just reviewing past memories is not enough. The memories and fantasies require new decisions about social perceptions, self- intentions and expectations.

Let us imagine treating a patient who tends to enter self-states with an irrational degree of bitterness towards the world. The therapist may use verbal techniques to clarify these excessively hostile feelings and the developmental experiences that led to repetitive angry and accusatory self-states. One example would be finding emerging evidence for a childhood sense of pervasive and persisting injustice and dissatisfaction. Hyper-vigilance for mistreatment can persist into adulthood and become a self-fulfilling prophecy that affects both current outside relationships as well as in-therapy transference states.

Transference feelings might be formulated by observing the patient repeatedly accusing the therapist for doing things poorly or incorrectly. Exploration of similar past feelings might lead to seeing a long-standing attitude of seeking compensation for past frustrations. The patient might even harbor a desire for revenge or compensation from others seen as frustrating or harmful in the past. This may be linked to a vague sense of guilt. Even though the fantasies of revenge may be warded-off, the patient may feel guilty of potential harm to the parental figure as if their angry thoughts were able to have produced bodily harm. The reconstruction in therapy reduces transference feelings, strengthens the alliance, and can lead to new narratives of the problem past and how the future could be different.

Perhaps as the therapist and patient make an effort to be explicit, the patient can say out loud that he believes that he has not been loved because at his core he is "unlovable." The patient may switch from the past to predicting the future, "No one will ever love me, but then why should anyone ever love me." An accusation can even be leveled in the present moment at the therapist, "And you can't help me with that. You haven't and you probably can't." The therapist might not challenge the transference accusation, instead moving to side with the patient, by saying something like, "I think I may understand you this way, there is an expectation that you will never be loved as you once wanted so desperately to be loved. That may make you speculate that you are somehow weak, dirty, and defective." This rather extreme statement clarifies implicit concepts and challenges the patient towards a more realistic, present-moment, self-appraisal.

Malcom

For example, Malcolm feared he was unlovable. Then, as an adolescent, he developed grandiose plans to win the Nobel Prize by discovering a cure for cancer. This plan became an obsession to prove that he would finally be worthy of love. The plan was a motivation for achievement, but falling short as an adult led to bouts of hopelessness, feelings of failure, and loneliness.

In his mind he also took a stance. He thought of himself being angry at his mentors and the support given his work as being insufficient to his needs. These present attitudes were then likened to memories of his past relationships with senior figures. Once the linkage was clear and agreed upon the therapist stayed on the topic, but asked that Malcolm switch his attention to the deployment of these negative attitudes into his projected future.

Did Malcolm want to change anything? As these discussions progressed, the therapist encouraged resetting goals from adolescent fantasies. Various goals were appraised for the future that seemed more attainable. This included narratives of taking steps towards potentially satisfying, and mature goals such as doing and teaching productive research methods, learning to obtain satisfaction from episodes of respect from colleagues and gratitude from trainees. Using these new value priorities, Malcolm reconsidered the present and new future, and how to move forward in a new way with his mentor.

Linking

By alternately linking past, present, and future time frames, explicit verbalizations are progressively advanced. This helps the patient remember new intentions for behavioral patterns. Repetition is essential, and observing what happens often modifies and improves formulations and leads to sharper techniques.

Often a maladaptive pattern has a function. Distressing self-states may still protect the patient from experiencing even more distressing self states. This layering is worth exploring.

If a patient is sulking or pouting for example, a therapist may ask: "What purpose might sulking serve?" A patient may give a vague answer. The therapist may then try to rephrase what the patient said in an interpretive manner.

Taking the patient's pronoun stance

Very often therapists tell patients, "You may be feeling . . ." Sometimes it works better to use "I" instead of "you," so instead of the therapist saying, "You like to feel justified and seeing the other person as unjust makes you feel better," the therapist can take the patient's pronoun stance and say something like: "I like feeling justified, and acting disgruntled verifies my sense of grievance and dissatisfaction with the world I have to live in." Saying "you" can feel like an accusation to a patient who is exquisitely vulnerable to criticism. Saying "I" rather than "you" can help the patient listen and focus more reflectively.

As just mentioned, unpleasant moods may trump even worse states of mind. For example, sulking tells another person that one does not feel fairly treated and that one wants more attention. Sulking can elicit attention, so it is preferable to despairing, which feels even worse. After evaluating the underlying emotions, an interpretation and attitude can be formulated. Once again, the therapist may venture a clarification by use of the patient's pronoun, taking the patient's stance. The therapist can say something like "When I sulk, my underlying purpose is to get you to apologize for not giving me what I wanted, and then to give me what I want."

Putting attitudes into self-talk helps a patient reassess the rationality and/or effectiveness of a particular stance. New scenarios can be imagined. The process in therapy helps the patient take an active and more mature role in planning how to behave instead of sulking.

The patient can be helped to form a new self-talk dialogue such as: "I am not going to get the attention I want from this person, but that does not mean I am a worthless or lost person (as I have tended to believe), or that this person is always going to be incapable of changing his behavior towards me." Once desires are clarified, a more assertive role can be learned. This can be put into words by role-playing various types of conversational scenarios in therapy to explore what to say when.

Reinforcement of new narratives of self

The patient might find it useful to repeat a particular phrase as an experiment. An insightful phrase could be something like: "I am going to do something I enjoy that makes me feel good about myself, and I will stop sulking and being pre-occupied with self-pity, and no longer worry about the frustrating memory of how I was neglected." Such a narrative can also be a future plan for doing something positive for someone else as a way of establishing a connection.

Complex insight

Interpretations may also introduce a patient to their own complexity. Many patients interpret a present-moment interpersonal situation according to several unconscious parallel processing role-relationship models (Kernberg, 1980; Knapp, 1991; Stinson, 1991; Horowitz, 2014). Each model elicits a different interpretation of the situation, which in turn produces different emotional responses. These script-like patterns do not emerge from full consciousness, but may arrive as premonitions; like Anna, a patient may consciously experience certain emotions without fully knowing why.

Once a patient has learned to express their feelings about a relationship in several complex ways, the therapist can help them reappraise what is happening during an ambivalent reaction. The patient can clarify the consequences of using projections and expectations from their long-standing models. The therapy process can then support the patient in learning more about forming stable relationships. Andre provides a suitably complex example.

Andre

Andre's behavior with women was often based on scenarios built on old and now inappropriate views of himself. The following example exhibits the techniques involved in progressing from clarifying patterns to forming new self-narratives. Presented here are three of Andre's core models of how he as a man might relate to a sexually desirable woman. Andre initially tended to shift his feelings, plans, and behaviors depending on the active relationship model. He worked in therapy to increase the harmony of his self-organization, create new narratives, and anticipate the new successful outcomes of these achievement in his future relationships with women.

Model #1: According to his chivalrous, romantic model, Andre was a good, heroic, and spiritually devoted person, who admired physically abstinent or "asexual" women. Although he may be romantically in love with her, he would restrain himself from sexual advances upon such a "pure woman." His inner critic gave him pride for this ethical stance.

Model #2: Another model he had of himself was as a Don Juan, who took advantage of a woman who would be unable to resist his sexual advances. He could seduce her into sexual encounters that she might otherwise refuse.

Model #3: Andre also had a weak self-schema, which was activated when he viewed himself involved with a powerful, dominating woman who could cast a spell on him, eventually smothering and trapping him. His reactive attitude would be to distance himself from caring about her and becoming entangled, thus avoiding the dangers of his self-critic assigning him shame for his "submissiveness."

These three role-relationship models operated implicitly in his preconscious mind, producing conscious representations of the self and other attributes carried forward into the present by his past development of these attitudes and their associated emotions. These implicit models were made more explicit by exploring stories about what had happened in several unsatisfactory romances. Talking with the therapist led to new, more cohesive self-narratives. In this way, Andre learned of his complexity in relationships. He began to see a repeated cycle of self-states.

Along the path of these insights, the therapist repeated suggestions of the value of observing what was going on in the present moment or in planning a date with a desirable woman. Andre found that he was making a number of assumptions, so the therapist suggested he investigate these assumptions by paying more attention, listening more carefully to actual verbal and non-verbal communication, and then describing them in words in the therapy conversations.

Andre learned to tell a kind of story about the cycle of his self-states, and how they were not in tune with his actual companions. In the beginning of several potential romantic relationships, Andre would approach a woman with many polite courtesies, thinking of her according to his romantic love model. In his fantasies, he would rescue her from a predatory rival, such as an abusive boyfriend, and she would admire and adore him. He would begin a sexual relationship with her, and then in his mind she would seem to morph from the desirable and devoted woman into a domineering and demanding woman who might trap him into a marriage he did not want.

To distance himself from the danger of being caught in a joyless commitment, he would begin a sexual relationship with someone else he did not care about, using her only as a sexual object. Infidelity would lead to a break-up with the strong, dangerous woman. In a cycle of self-states, his self-concept changed from the role of hero-rescuer to that of a weak victim. His wish-fear dilemma started with the desire for a loving and sensuous relationship of commitment, but with too strong a threat of consequences represented by his fear that the woman he might love would be like a spider, ensnaring him in her web.

Andre learned through the use of reflective self-awareness and the conversations in the therapeutic alliance to reappraise not only what was happening, but also what alternatively might happen. As his preemptory defenses against the danger of being trapped were reduced, the therapy itself was experienced as more secure; Andre was able to correct his attitudes by gradually being more open to new possible experiences.

He advanced his self-narrative by forming a more adaptive, flexible observation of how the women in his life actually behaved. He learned to observe that they felt sexual, self-controlled, and equal to him, rather than either subordinate or superior to him. His irrational attitudes changed slowly, resulting from his new determination to carefully observe and reflect while experimenting with closer encounters in his day-to-day life.

Encouraged by his success in actual relationships, Andre learned more realistic views of himself and broadened his understanding of the complex roles women and men can take with each other in different states of mind. Eventually, he was able to overcome his limited approach to relationships and had a realistic chance to learn from bolder connections, albeit with some inner sense of risk. His story of the future defined goals for succeeding step-by-step in career, marriage, and parenthood.

Adam: Parallel processing of social interactions

Adam, a graduate student in physics, provides another example of promoting growth in self-narratives. Adam was long overdue getting his doctorate because he kept procrastinating in writing his thesis. He consulted periodically with his supervising thesis professor, yet he often delayed status reports of his work. Procrastination jeopardized his career, and he sought help from a psychotherapist to get past the dangerous pattern of avoiding potential advancement in his work.

During discussions with his psychotherapist, Adam received help with clarifying what was going on in his mind about his relationship with his own work as well as with his thesis advisor. In a state related to his work, Adam's self-concepts were competent and his expectations of his supervisor were of mutual positive regard. Unfortunately, unconscious triggers either from within or based on his perceptions of his supervisor, sometimes caused Adam to organize his experiences according to other less useful schemas.

For example, if the professor seemed impatient and abrupt with him, Adam shifted into a self-state of ruminative worry about his own possible incompetence. In this model, he viewed himself as a child interacting with a harshly critical authority figure. He expected the authority figure to label his shortcomings in such a scornful way that Adam would give up.

Most of the time, Adam was in either the working state or the state of ruminative worry. The more he delayed, the more he worried. However, two other states occasionally emerged. One was a self-state of excited fantasy, in which he imagined that he was a great scientist illuminating a problem for his professor. Adam fantasized that he could solve an important scientific problem that his professor could not, thereby catapulting himself to fame.

At other times, Adam viewed himself as aggrieved. In this scenario, the teacher would fail to meet Adam's expectations, and Adam would complain to others with a whining attitude. In this state, he felt justified in complaining because he felt his teacher should do the necessary intellectual work for him. If and when Adam recognized this behavior, he felt disgusted with himself for whining so much and experiencing a combination of inappropriate ingratitude and an overly dependent self-concept.

Adam's repertoire included four self-images: (1) sincere student in the working state, (2) incompetent child in the worried state, (3) great scientist in the excited fantasy state, and (4) needy, deprived child in the whining state. By clarifying and challenging these implicit self-narratives, Adam was able to harmonize them into supraordinate views of himself as flexibly processing different potential self-states. This increased his confidence in achieving better and more realistic self-appraisals in the future.

By paying close attention to the differences between his old attitudes and the realities of the student–professor and patient–therapist situations, Adam became capable of having franker, safer experiences of negotiation. He stabilized himself in his working state and developed more competent career plans.

Summary

Evidence of avoidant maneuvers and intrusive emotions indicate topics worthy of closer formulation. In conversations about these topics, patient and therapist work together to clarify active self-schemas at play that are in fact obsolete. New self-narratives are formed verbally, making implicit beliefs more explicit, so they can be challenged with new observations and reappraisals. The therapist then assists the patient in exploring possible selves in the future.

A frame analysis connecting past, present, and future self-concepts helps the patient gain insight and the capacity for self-reflective awareness. Such analyses often involve clearly stated interpretations and reconstructions by the therapist. These remarks are gently suggested as possibilities of formulation. The constructs and contexts may be repeated and revised to better fit new observations of how the patient reacted to previous conceptualizations. When the therapist conceptualizes for the patient, the patient is expected to use this as an opportunity for reassessment. That includes challenges to what the therapist said as well as revisions and re-narrations of their own. The goal is for the patient to own their identity narrative.

In this section on growth in identity coherence and continuity over time, we have touched on a number of topics. Safety reduces the threat of self-exposures in therapy. As danger subsides, defenses diminish and self-understanding improves. Obstacles to change are surmounted and new self-narratives are hatched. Patients learn a new story of identity and relationships across various periods of their life. Importantly, they increase self-esteem and form a more realistic set of future plans.

Relationships

This section expands on some of the issues of how self is embedded in roles of relationship and scenarios reflecting limitations in enhancing connections with others. The formulations of common patterns from schemas formed in early development are advanced in Chapter 5 on Changing Relationship Patterns. Chapter 6 discusses techniques for enrichment of relationship capacities and Chapter 7 refers specifically to deepening sexual relationships.

5

Changing relationship patterns

This chapter expands on common patterns that clinicians find when observing and formulating why patients repeat maladaptive relationships or fail to develop relationships. An important aspect of formulation will be on understanding how past relationships affect present maladaptive patterns. The goals of the techniques discussed are to promote more satisfying and adaptive ways of relating to others in the future.

Observation

By taking a detailed history, the clinician can elicit relevant complaints and limitations such as repeated failures to sustain a friendship or complete a work task. The patient may bring up current concerns, often about relationships at work or at home, sometimes about the terrible loneliness that accompanies a lack of meaningful relationships. The therapist's observations should emphasize the stance that a patient assumes in interpersonal transactions, as well as the emotional responses and reactions that occur within the patient's mind.

The words used repeatedly by the patient may help the therapist in formulating patterns. For example, words like feeble, devious, exploitative, vexed, snide, controlling, emotionally constipated, and worthless may be heard over and over again. Such words may help formulation of roles and attributes in repetitive maladaptive interpersonal patterns.

Patient reports of previous critical adverse experiences, real or imagined, may involve failures, strains, traumas, losses, and deficiencies in relationships. The therapist observes the patient's states of mind as these stories are told, noting any entry into under-modulated states. The therapist also observes the point, in relating a story, where a patient deflects from frank disclosure in order to avoid emerging emotions. At that point the patient may move from a well-modulated to an over-modulated state.

If the therapeutic alliance creates a safe enough space to do so, the patient can express feelings and remain longer in well-focused conversations. As a patient learns how the therapist listens, the patient in turn is learning how to listen to others by an unconscious identification with the therapist. As the therapist observes this, they may encourage the patient to describe their inner experience of being with the therapist and how that experience differs from what it was like when therapy first began. The therapist can aid observation by asking alternately silently and aloud, "Are we talking more frankly or are we moving towards a distant, less communicative relationship?"

As enrichment of the alliance occurs, the patient may report asking him- or herself between sessions: "What might Dr. Smith say?" The patient starts to link topics addressed in the sessions to episodes of everyday life. The therapist may also observe that the patient becomes more aware of the therapist as a human being in the professional framework, and how he or she intends to help the patient.

Formulation

Formulation about relationship patterns often involves looking for role-relationship models that may underlie the pattern of maladaptive transactions. The individual's repertoire of self-other beliefs will have developed in personality structure as a product of generalizations from past experiences. Some of these are appropriate organizers for thinking about current relationships, but some are not. The reason is that former generalizations from interpersonal experiences into cognitive maps were made by immature minds, minds often developing in complex and difficult situations (Chefetz, 2015; Young, Klosko & Weishaar, 2006).

Let us consider the emergence of a dormant role-relationship model into a present problem, where formulation helped the patient reduce a fear of being out of control. As a person becomes a parent, his or her latent child–parent role models may become reactivated. Sometimes that can occur with roles reversed, with the individual identifying with the parent role. This reactivation may occur no matter how much the patient disliked the treatment he or she received as a child, as was the case with Sharon and her three-year-old daughter, Annie.

The power struggle between Sharon and Annie

One day, Annie was coloring in the kitchen while her mother, Sharon, was organizing some papers for work. The little girl wanted to imitate her mother. She grabbed some of the mother's papers. Sharon asked her to stop, saying: "These are mommy's papers and you have to leave them alone."

When Annie continued pulling at the papers, Sharon repeated her remark more firmly. Annie ignored her mother and kept on. Sharon shifted into an under-modulated state and screamed shrilly at Anne, who burst into tears and wailed. Sharon then felt a searing remorse. She cried and hugged Annie very hard.

When Sharon was a child, her mother had screamed at her and, out of control, hit her hard when she was disobedient. She had continued to do so until Sharon was a teenager, when Sharon had threatened to hit her mother back if she did not stop. Sharon always hated this sudden surge of temper in her mother, and had vowed to her dolls during play that it would never happen to them. Of course she promised herself that she would never be abusive to her own children. Then, faced with work pressures and a deadline, she had acted harshly and quickly like her mother. The ingrained pattern manifested automatically when the situation triggered it. Sharon brought this up right away in therapy because she wanted to work on restraining this automatic response tendency.

Sharon became aware of another problematic reaction to her daughter. According to this pattern, she found herself resenting Annie after they had an especially good time together and she had showered Annie with kindness and generosity. Although Annie did express appreciation and love her mother, sometimes Annie's affection did not seem to be enough of a reward for Sharon.

What Sharon was actually resenting was not consciously clear to her for some time. Then Sharon realized that she resented the fact that Annie had a better mother than she herself had experienced. Astonishingly, with help from interpretations based on formulations, Sharon realized that she felt a rivalry with Annie for receiving what her own mother had seemed to deny her. Understanding that concept helped Sharon control her attitudes and emotions. Her goal for the future was clear: to try to be as good a mother as possible to Annie and not repeat her own childhood grievance. Sharon could learn to just enjoy Annie as her daughter, without rivalry and envy, living in the true present.

Roles of self and other in transferences and therapeutic alliances

As discussed in previous chapters, some definitions are helpful to this relationship pattern aspect of a case formulation. A *therapeutic alliance* is a model of roles and transactions that each party in therapy learns to expect from the other. It builds on experiences between therapist and patient. The therapist is offering aspects of the framework such as non-critical stance, unconditional positive regard, and supportive listening. The patient learns by identifying with this stance, and coming to expect it from the therapist.

The patient intends to learn from the therapy experience and from the therapist. But the patient is also offering, perhaps at times provoking, other bids for relationship roles that are not therapeutic in intention. These bids are sometimes enactments of the past that lead to transference feelings. The therapist can formulate what a patient seems to be appraising about the situation, and what leads into activation of transference feelings. The therapist formulates transference as one way of understanding the unconscious role-relationship models of a patient, which can help clarify a pattern of relationship problems outside therapy (Milrod, 1997; Busch et al., 2015; McWilliams, 2011; Cabaniss, 2010; Gabbard, 2014).

Some common patterns evolve out of difficult childhood attachments. As in previous chapters, I will discuss a few developmental problems that can lead the patient towards transference re-enactments. The general forms can lead to individualized formulations. Some common role-relationship models persist from early childhood fears of abandonment and we will start there.

Excessive fear of abandonment

All children have moments when their needs, wishes, desires, and requests are not instantly met. They learn to accept and tolerate such conditions and are taught such realities by consistent parents. With inconsistent parenting, a child may feel neglected while longing for a more secure attachment. The child can be frustrated and angry that an immediate need for care is not met. Moreover, the child may feel terrified over possible or actual abandonment by a principle caretaker.

If a child has experienced fearful separations, he or she may develop a self-schema of being an abandoned child pining for an absent caregiver. In the relationship model, the child may attribute powerful non-verbal emotions to the other. The child may view the other as withholding, or the self as worthless. This model may be deposited as a schema even if the felt neglect was due to a parental death or mental disorder such as withdrawal and apathy from a serious depression. A child with negative self-attributes may even assume that the parent died or became apathetically bed-ridden because the child was bad in some way.

Now as an adult, such a history of frustration can lead to a wish-fear-defense configuration of role-relationship models. The wish to be a worthwhile child receiving nurture from a loving other is one model. The fear of hopeless neediness of self in relation to another who rejects the supplicating self is another. A defensive role-relationship model in the overall configuration may schematize the self as alone, without expectations, and embittered and depressed because the world is empty. This model, painful as it seems, is somewhat protective against a persisting terror of separation.

Such configurations can dispose the patient to certain kinds of transference feelings, even a pathological and paradoxical rejection of the therapist's offers of support in the therapeutic alliance. Despite the therapist's clear offer of caring, a patient may become hostile and bitter as he or she nonetheless expects rejection and abandonment from the therapist. While the negative affect threatens the alliance, understanding the safety of the alliance can permit working through the transference feelings of hostility.

Passivity as an attachment strategy

The child in relation to an inconsistent parent may become passive and obedient to elicit desired attention. All actions conform to what the parental figure wants in order to avoid feeling the threat of abandonment. The situation may seem quiet, non-turbulent, and devoid of interpersonal conflicts, but the very safety of this role-relationship model can program the child for a lifetime of limited self-assertion.

In therapy, the passive behavior may have been observed as a pattern of mild but persistent complaining with minimal participation in exploring or enhancing plans. The patient awaits guidance. When this pattern of low initiative and leaving action up to the therapist is clarified, it may help for the patient to understand why it once seemed useful. Then patient is encouraged to take a more active role. Once more self-assertion is learned with the therapist, more assertive actions in outside situations can be planned. For example, the patient can learn to disagree diplomatically with a parent, spouse, friend, or supervisor, looking out in an enlightened way for his or her own best interests.

Rivalry

Competition is a healthy part of most societies. Some patients have difficulty in situations where rivalry is present. They may have a role-relationship model in which, in competition, one person is always harmed by the winner. Some children have difficulty controlling strong feelings of rivalry with a parent, sibling, or peer. At the extreme, a wish to get rid of a rival may also make someone feel like a bad person if they are admonished harshly for their thoughts. If so, the person can develop an exaggerated view of competition as being potentially harmful to others.

For example, a person may maintain the childhood belief that when one needy child gets attention, the other needy person is devalued. When this belief prevails, the person may resent another for expressing a desire for attention and need for care.

Pathological self-soothing

Children identify with their parents even if the parental figures fluctuate wildly in their behavior. If the parent handles stress by abusing recreational drugs or alcohol, engaging in promiscuous sex, or chain smoking, the child may see any of those behaviors as adaptive, strong, self-soothing responses to frustrating situations. Patterns of abuse of substances can rest upon such early models. Once such formulations are individualized to the actual patient, the consequences of such negative behaviors can be examined in therapy and less excessive self-soothing behaviors can be suggested as alternatives.

Excessive attention seeking

When a child experiences inconsistent care from a vital parental figure, and receives more attention when he or she gets into trouble, falls ill, or is injured, the child may learn to exhibit personal suffering in order to receive care. Later in life, presentation of distress and enfeeblement can become an unconscious tool to satisfy a need for more attention. The child learns that, although parents can punish and reward, they too can be made to feel miserable by the child's actions, especially when the child complains and pouts. The child realizes that the parents may give in to the child's demands as a means of reducing their own distress from the child's negative expressions. The child realizes his power to manipulate the parent. If such patterns are noted in therapy, and developmental histories allow such a formulation, the clinician can illustrate what function the behavior is aimed to achieve, and suggest better ways to create moments of closeness in relationships.

Harsh inner critics

A parent who struggles to avoid self-disgust and social shame may obscure his or her own role as a participant during troubled times, and instead place all the responsibility for the problem on the child. By always blaming the child, the parent can feel superior and may even derive pleasure from expressing deprecatory criticism. Repeated interactions of this sort lead the child to develop both a degraded self-concept and to make harsh self-judgments.

A related behavior from a patient with such schemas is to express embarrassment or even self-disgust as an appeasement when they fail to please others. The adult with this trait operates in a state of hyper-vigilance to the expected stress of doing something wrong in the eyes of others. Sometimes traits of perfectionism and emotional over-modulation persist.

As adults, patients with harsh internal criticism strive in vain for success in what they do. They may develop compulsions to repeat over and over, trying for goals that are too ideal to reach. If they don't reach a goal, it means oneself is to blame. An adult tendency to deliver harsh shaming statements can be the result.

Technique

Patients may learn from formulations of how maladaptive interpersonal patterns originated. The chronically bitter attitudes of some children, when enacted, undermine their chances for intimacy. They may develop compulsions to repeat over and over, trying for goals that are intended to master childhood problems, but in ways that disrupt relationships instead of enriching connections.

Fears of abandonment may be compensated by hyper-alertness for rejection. Desires for closeness are concealed by a stance of being aloof, to prevent the shame of not being sufficiently accepted. When enacted in therapy, the avoidant and suspicious relationship pattern of a patient with excessive fears of potential abandonment is defensive. Clarification of the overall pattern can occur in several contexts, or one of the several contexts where the patient can best consciously recognize the attitudes. That is the layer of aloofness while hoping for connection but expecting rejection can be identified in current outside relationships, in the past of memories of relationships, and/or in the present context of the therapy transactional opportunities and expectations.

Memories of feeling as if abandoned, or actually bereft of attachment, can be painful to recollect, even if that is a helpful clarification of a past to present linkage. Sometimes it is helpful to focus attention, perhaps repeatedly, on memories when help and compassion were given by some prior figure (Lieberman et al., 2005). Such a memory or even a fantasy version of such a memory can activate positive role-relationship models and promote that expectation and self-presentation in current contexts. That activation in the present moment can reduce bitterness towards anyone who seems about to be rejecting, a bitterness that can provoke a rejection, in a paradoxical manner.

Therapy techniques with such patients should aim resolutely, patiently, and repetitively at modifying attitudes of exaggerated negative expectations. For example, the therapist should be alert to the patient becoming suspicious of betrayal. The therapist may, in some transference states, be seen as having behaviors recognized by the patient as a prelude to abandonment. As already mentioned, as a defense against the danger of being abandoned, the patient may abandon the therapist by stopping treatment. To protect self-esteem, the patient acts to become the first to leave the relationship, rather than to be deflated by seeing the other as leaving first. If the therapist can interpret the reasons for the patient's urge to leave the therapist, a disruption of treatment may be prevented.

Sometimes having a clear interpretation of how and why the past has continued to operate in the present serves as a strong motivator to continue the slow work of change. Recognizing the source of bad moods leads to clearer and more reasoned plans for new experiential actions within social relationships. Understanding the developmental basis of a maladaptive pattern of social cognition and action may involve reprocessing childhood memories and fantasies.

Looking at these often traumatic memories and fantasies is to some extent desensitization of what may have previously been emotionally too intense or painful to contemplate. Some experiences from the past are being verbalized for the first time during this therapy, supported by communication with a trusted other. Technically, the focus of attention becomes the near future, as the therapist leans towards how the pattern may change for the better.

Chet: A passive-aggressive pattern

Chet was working on his goals for increasing his work satisfaction and salary during a middle phase of his psychotherapy. His complaints included a mild but unremitting sense of personal failure. One episode proved very illuminating.

An administrative assistant to a top executive, Chet was asked to switch to work full-time with another executive whose secretary was on leave. The new superior demanded high-quality work which Chet lapsed in doing. The therapist asked for details of what happened.

The executive gave Chet many tasks and he, feeling irritated at the burden, carried them out incompletely and with slight errors. When asked for a fast completion, Chet did his assignment very slowly and without interest. If he completed the tasks, he remained idle instead of taking on other obvious subsequent tasks.

The executive became increasingly irritated and repeated clear instructions and deadlines. Chet did not change. The superior finally lost her temper and scolded Chet after he had missed the deadline for the letter, and also used the interdepartmental green stationery for the important outside letter and Chet knew he should have done it on white paper. In the argument that followed, the executive became impatient and angry, and revealed that she had doubts about Chet. He, in turn, acted as though he was extremely hurt by what she said. Chet complained widely and threatened to file a hostile-work place grievance, saying that he had been harshly castigated for a trivial error, and that she had given him poor supervision.

Feeling threatened by a possible Human Resource review of a complaint against her, the executive became scrupulously courteous to him, tolerating his poor performance and his sullen demeanor, while documenting his errors and low productivity level. Chet realized that losing his position soon was a possibility, but his pattern continued. He was often sullen, and other people remained ambivalent about him, blocking the possibility of a promotion.

The therapist decided to give a long response in segments that Chet might contemplate, watching how Chet was taking each phrase to see if he could focus on what the therapist intended, or would get irritated by the intervention. The therapist said, "I think we can understand that you felt demeaned in the new situation and became moody and irritable." Chet nodded and waited for more. The therapist continued, "There may be a pattern there that we should look at closely. If I am right about this, you seem to have a strategy of getting back at your boss by using covert sabotage efforts." The therapist raised his eyebrows and offered Chet a questioning face, as if asking if he should continue. Chet listened in a well-modulated state.

The therapist continued the interpretation, "It seems that now because of her outburst of reactive anger at you, she must act nice to avoid a grievance procedure. But while she backed off, our focus here is on a pattern you repeat, which can be a self-defeating one in the long run even though you made her feel embarrassment."

Chet was silent for a bit then said, "I don't quite get the pattern you mean." The therapist said, "I think I have noticed in your stories about work especially, that when you get frustrated you feel irritated with someone superior to you. You do not negotiate through the problem directly but instead frustrate them as by slowly doing something you could get done more swiftly. They do get frustrated and may even over-react. You seem to score a point, but it is not in your enlightened best interest. The bosses may even call you passive-aggressive."

Chet realized that he could do better than to go on repeating this pattern and asked for advice. The therapist said: "You know, I think we might go back over some of those situations, like that time you threatened to file a grievance complaint. We can both comment on what seemed to be going on, and we can go forward and imagine what might happen if the same type of confrontation and mutual frustration happens in the future. I have a hunch you can learn to communicate tactfully at the moment and negotiate a way through your sense of frustration."

Chet tried to clarify in words the memory of what had happened in exchanges with the executive. He revised a plan for how he might handle a future repetition of the situation. He rehearsed in therapy sessions how to speak about his frustrations to the executive in a way that was both assertive and respectful. His bitterness cooled, as did his fear of being fired. He felt proud that he was learning. As a result of learning more adaptive assertiveness and responsibility, he was later promoted to a supervisory position.

Morgan: Learning, from a narcissistic position

Morgan came to psychotherapy for help with his chronic anxiety and tension. He was nearly 40 and had no lasting relationships for over a decade. Understanding his development of self and other role-relationship models became a process that he valued because it opened his eyes to 1) understanding himself more gently from the self-critic's role, 2) increasing efforts to empathize with others, and 3) observing the fact that others sometimes had empathy for him.

Morgan had talents in entertaining his parents. In telling his stories of childhood, a permeating theme was that Morgan's mother doted on him. His childhood role of being special did not gradually decline, as it does for most cherished children. Instead, Morgan maintained the illusion of his near-godlike status. He intended to get all he felt he was entitled to, and he expected others to somehow know these desires and provide gratification of his wishes.

His self-narrative about the past expanded and revised as his childhood memories were remembered and discussed in therapy. Childhood memories from the time before going to school seemed blissful. As his worldview expanded, he learned in school that while he was gifted in certain ways, other children were sometimes older, brighter, stronger, and more competent than him. Admitting that he was not always admired and not always the center of attention made him feel vulnerable, so he wanted others to see him as a star as he had been used to in his early years. However, others tended to ignore his bluster and he felt stressed by the banter or peer rejections.

To bolster this star self-concept, he used his large weekly allowance to purchase gifts for potential friends. Unfortunately, those friends merely took advantage of him because, in spite of the bribes, they did not allow him to take control of the flow of activities. Internally, he cherished a grandiose self-concept, but the lack of reflection on his worth as a companion left him lonely. He did have many talents, and did develop the related skills. So he did well in school, he finished college, and started what could be a good career.

Now, as an adult at work and with his roommate, he continued the old pattern, but realized that even the roommate wanted more than his rent and shared domestic chores. Friendship was missing. Also, he was starting to feel the need to go beyond superficial dating towards something that could lead to marriage.

He felt unable to make any progress towards these goals of being a better friend, much less an intimate partner and eventual father. He sought therapy and the topic of concern quickly became attention to understanding relationships, especially as he attempted new connections with new people. As stories were told, the therapist experimented with interrupting him by asking what he thinks he expected to happen next in the situation, at that point in time. This experiment had good results: Morgan seemed to look back into his mind and try to figure out what he had expected to happen, and then reappraised those ideas.

When Morgan began to look at himself, he recognized that he was still expecting to be living in the protective cocoon of his childhood showered with unending admiration. He wanted people to roll out the red carpet upon his arrival and in therapy felt himself to be the therapist's very special, prize patient.

Once there was an urgent situation involving another patient that caused the therapist to be late to Morgan's session. That made Morgan feel that he was not special, and that was very irritating to him. Morgan recognized and reported his irritation. He figured out that this was a repetition of expecting to be "the special one." This experience contrasted with his realistic understanding that the therapist must have other patients whose care was equally important. Still, that contrast of attitudes was a struggle within his own mind. Sometimes he fell silent in mid-sentence and looked away from the therapist.

At this time, the therapist repeated inquiries of what he was thinking, and asked him to imagine what the therapist might be thinking. These inquiries slowed down his emotional reactions and led him to accept that he was not the therapist's only prime, prized patient. This process led to a reduction in transference feelings and an improved therapeutic alliance. The topic of which patient got more or less attention from the therapist led to further expansion of the network of Morgan's ideas. Morgan was able to start revealing many relationship stories involving both work and dating. In all of these stories he seemed to be preoccupied with keeping score of who got what from whom.

The therapist called this to his attention and suggested that in looking towards the future, " Perhaps we could consider that your next relationships can build towards more mutuality than this scorekeeping arrangement. I think that work on that can help with your tendency to either get angry or frightened when the score seems unequal."

Morgan had a tendency to align his attention towards sources of either praise or blame. Because of work on the therapeutic alliance, he had already learned that the therapist was not blaming him for his "tendency to either get angry or frightened," and was not praising him for being finished with a growth process. The wording of the therapist's remark was positive in saying that work could be done and improvements already made could continue.

The new experience of listening to the therapist listening to him helped him modify his general interpersonal expectations. He also listened more to others: hearing carefully their offers and their needs, he gradually reduced his sense of entitlement to their undivided attention to him and only him. His categories for understanding others, as with the therapist, expanded from the limiting dichotomies of "Either praise me or you are blaming me."

Bert: Courting failure by procrastinating

Bert, a dental student, struggled with power and control issues. Although he did well in his courses, he had difficulty with authority figures. At times he seemed to be competitive with the therapist. When dating, he engaged in power struggles that women found irritating because he always wanted to be in control. His dominance over shared activities led relationships to flounder. He was not able to maintain any relationship for long, not even friendships.

The consequences of his attitude were especially grave in his dentistry program. Bert was now in danger of failing school. His supervisor evaluated him and found his paperwork substandard. All the students complained about completing the many records and forms, but Bert was seen as rebellious and disrespectful. He challenged the details of the required paperwork as unnecessary and hampering educational time.

Realizing he was close to losing sight of his career goals, and having been advised that his behavior was an issue, Bert sought psychotherapy. He told his therapist that he sometimes felt that doing the reports was irrelevant to both providing good patient care and gaining instruction for himself. He knew rationally that it was necessary for the survival of the clinic that payment for services was obtained through completion of the insurance reports. However, when he sat down at the computer to fill out the electronic record, he felt as if he was weakly submitting to the authority of his supervisor and wasting his own time.

When asked by the supervisor to bring his patients' electronic records up to date, he sometimes complied submissively, but at other times turned stubbornly neglectful, belligerent, and sour. In the latter case, he immediately felt that he had gone too far and shifted into an over-controlled, seemingly subservient state of mind in which he apologized. The instructor was irritated with both his resistance and his obsequious submission.

Bert tried hard to make himself do the reports, setting up times and schedules for this task. Seated in front of a computer, with his fingers on the keys and his notes at hand, his thoughts shifted elsewhere. Trying to refocus, he sometimes saw himself as capitulating meekly, slavishly filling out boxes about diagnoses and procedures. He then felt as if he was not masterfully treating his patients, but only obtaining money for the clinic. Bert procrastinated, allowing a great many reports to become past due.

Bert liked to feel like an idealist moving decisively ahead with excellent treatments and procedures without submitting to bureaucratic nonsense. On the other hand, he could see his refusal to fill out the forms as a sign of poor performance. In a dream, he appeared before a faculty committee and was exposed as a child pretending in play to be a dentist.

Bert reported that, as a child, he had felt too controlled by one of his parents. He had stubbornly resisted the domineering demands, and his parent had then backed down, letting Bert gain control. From these interactions, Bert learned a tactic of continually thwarting authority figures, attempting to reverse who was in the power role and gaining the upper hand by stubborn refusals of their demands. However, this strategy failed him in adult life. Interpretation of the apparent success of the strong defiant childhood pattern helped Bert attend to the differences between then, now, and the near future.

The dialogue and clarifications of therapy helped him identify his current pattern of struggling for power instead of doing his work. When the therapist tried to alter the focus of their discussion, Bert might alter his focus and talk about the topic the therapist suggested, but with an overtone of sarcasm projecting that he considered this focus ridiculous. He would enter over-modulated states. He would then either insincerely aim at proving that the therapist's suggestion was philosophically foolish or just continue as if the therapist had not spoken.

The therapist repeated remarks such as this: "You seem distant from me right now, and to be moving even further away. I wonder if you're doing that to get away from conflicting ideas that either you or I have to be the top dog in this moment. I think there is a middle ground of cooperating without either of us needing to be in control of the other. I think that might be worth working toward." Bert began to see that it could be possible to choose together with the therapist where best to place attention in the moment. That negotiation did not have to be some kind of argument. Cooperation seemed like a new possibility! He began to revise his understanding of what could go on between people. In particular, Bert found hope in the idea of equal partners or cooperating teacher–trainee relationships.

Bert's type of power struggle was enacted in therapy as tension around who was in control of choosing the agenda. The therapist avoided being too insistent (too strong) or too non-directive (too weak) in choosing where to pay attention. He calmly, rather than critically, said what he observed. He sketched out what could possibly now happen and how cooperation occurs by give and take.

Role-relationship models can be advanced by new experiences. Along the way, insight can assist in developing new motivations and plans. This insight is deepened as the original reasons for present maladaptive patterns are explored. This process clarifies the implicit ideas behind felt emotions and emotional self-states. Emotions are clarified as the patterns are examined in terms of attributions of self and other, and the expected "map" of action, reaction, and response to the reaction are examined. Once cumbersome or inappropriate attitudes are clarified, alternatives can be suggested as part of the learning process.

Summary

Complex patterns may occur in a repeated cycle that forms part of a patient's maladaptive pattern in interpersonal relationships. A therapist's observation of how one set of attitudes shifts to another may lead to the formulation of cycles. A cycle may begin with a situation that activates a patient's wish, leading to arousal of the patient's latent fear of certain consequences, which in turn activates an avoidant role-relationship model. The cycle repeats when the wish remains ungratified. The propensity to repeat the cycle can be formulated as a configuration of desired, dreaded, and compromising role-relationship models. Useful techniques are ones that consider alternative relationship negotiations, breaking the cycle.

6

Advancing relationship capacities

Healthy close relationships involve a feeling of mutuality, as well as a shared understanding that both parties intend to remain constant over time. Successful exploratory psychotherapy that supports personality growth can enhance a patient's capacity to form satisfying relationships. Supportive psychotherapies can lead to enhanced relationships through the use of psychoeducation and advice. Both supportive and exploratory psychotherapies require new kinds of relationship trials outside the therapeutic relationship.

In exploratory psychotherapy, especially, the patient is learning to trust the therapist with unusual for the patient levels of frank self-exposure and feelings. This learning process builds from an initial therapeutic alliance to a tested, new form of therapeutic alliance. For many patients this is a new relationship experience and aspects of it can be used as the patient tries to modify behaviors and experiences outside of the therapy relationship (Renick, 2006; Britton et al., 2011; Goldfried and Davilla, 2005; Levenson, 2010; Norcross and Wampol, 2011).

This chapter discusses experiences of increasing levels of connection between the patient and the therapist in the therapeutic alliance. Empathic communication within sessions can increase the patient's capacity for understanding and lead to the patient becoming more empathic in other relationships. Identifying and analyzing negative transference reactions can ameliorate the attitudes and decrease negative feelings both within and outside of the therapeutic relationship (Aron, 1996; Bohleber et al., 2013).

Observation

The therapist observes patterns in the various relationships described by the patient and asks questions to elicit specific information that will help the therapist and the patient understand why relationships stagnate or rupture. Similar relationship problems often manifest in the relationship that the patient has with the therapist, at least in some states of mind. The therapist observes how in moments of transference reactions the patient seems to be feeling toward the therapist.

Ideally, a therapist is also alert to his or her counter-transference reactions toward the patient. As a test of the safety of the therapeutic situation, a patient may test the therapist, as with certain provocative verbalizations or physical movements and displays. The therapist may observe provocations and also may observe his or her own psychological or bodily reaction. Added observations in this context may help in inferring how the patient may be behaving with others outside of therapy and how others in these situations might react to the patient.

The therapist also observes when the patient seems to be moving emotionally closer or further away from the therapist. What situational characteristic might be triggering the patient to move to a more distant inter-personal position in regard to expressing emotion? Answering that question may explain why the patient seems to become more remote.

Formulation

The therapeutic relationship provides invaluable information about outside relationships. The patient may feel positive feelings towards the therapist and this may represent a wish for ideal parenting that did not occur in childhood. This positive transference may be transient and turn to negative feelings under certain circumstances, for example if the therapist is perceived as uninterested or withdrawn by the patient (Høglend et al., 2011; Clarkin et al., 2006; Horowitz and Möller, 2009).

Positive and negative transference reactions are based on attitudes that may have been developed in much earlier and more dependent relationships, or the lack of care when truly needful. Children who have experienced early stressful events may need close connection in current crises and rather depending on their own coping efforts as adults may irrationally idealize a potentially restorative person, to derive strength and hope from associating with that person. This may sooth them. Losing such a figure may revive states of hopelessness, bitterness, and fear.

The tendency to idealize can lead to irrational degrees of trust rather than accurate appraisals of the intentions and potential constancy of others in a close relationship. If so, it holds its own potential for frustration and deflation when the idealized person does not meet the patient's expectations. The relationship then feels broken, and all the positive feelings associated with the other may turn to rage at being let down. Formulation of this kind of dynamic can explain sometimes explosive changes in state from positive to negative transference feelings.

It may be helpful for the patient and therapist to formulate together, and to reconstruct how negative attitudes are formed. For example, as an abused child the patient may have identified with the role of aggressor as a means of coping with a vulnerable and dependent relationship position. A process of role reversal (identifying with the strong abusive parent) may allow this child to justify degrading or harming others as an adult. This may be manifested as feelings of scorn for the therapist for foolishly hoping for a relationship with the patient that would be more trusting and in alliance than the early relationship patterns with the sometimes caring and sometimes abusive parent.

When a child experiences repeated adverse events that lead to states of severe and protracted stress, they are more likely to have subsequent dissociative experiences, and feel a sense of disconnection from others. This may manifest itself in the relationship with the therapist. Damaged children may see themselves as both victim and aggressor, switching between states organized by these two roles. Disorganized and inconsistent attachment results. This has been reported in up to 80% in children with a history of maltreatment (Carlson, Ciccetti, Barnett, & Braunwald, 1989; Lyons-Ruth, 1996; Steele & Steele, 2008).

Inconsistent attitudes towards the therapist can be formulated as a pattern of emotional shifts. A patient may feel infatuated with a therapist and imagine that the therapist will provide a relationship of loving guidance. The patient wants constancy of care; suddenly transference feelings of hostility emerge when these hopes seem dashed. The patient may want to punish the therapist, by resisting the chance to change, and sabotaging the therapist's efforts. The therapist observes that he or she feels devalued and ineffective. The therapist can formulate the reasons for the obstacles to progress. Several techniques may be required to improve the therapeutic alliance so as to master these extreme shifts in emotional closeness.

Technique

The patient and the therapist are gradually identifying conflicted topics and finding various aspects of repetitive and maladaptive interpersonal patterns. Aspects of these patterns may occur in the therapy situation. Confrontation and clarification are helpful techniques when a therapeutic alliance is strong and resilient. Emerging emotions without clear ideational connections may be important to hold in consciousness and conversation for a time beyond the patient's inclination to move to some other topic.

A useful technique is to encourage the patient to observe and discuss what is going on in the present moment. Progress can be made as the therapist suggests that some of these observations of the therapist as made by the patient may be inaccurate or distorted appraisals, and that the patient may make similar interpretations of other people's intentions in outside relationships. The therapist may then encourage the patient to consider how the motives, reactions, and role-relationship models related to these distortions may have occurred in past relationships. As already mentioned, this technique works best when there is discussion and understanding of both roles in the therapeutic alliance role-relationship model.

A general format of a therapeutic alliance, conceptualized as roles of patient and therapist and expected transactions, is shown in Figure 6.1. One can compare and contrast such a role-relationship model with the pattern of self- and other beliefs that lead to obstacles in therapy or to transference feelings.

The therapist can offer a patient new ways of thinking about relationships. This can be a valuable aspect of psychoeducation insofar as it involves outside relationships examined as patterns in therapy. What is going on in an outside relationship may be displaced and enacted towards the therapist, in some states of mind. These may help the therapist infer what the patient wishes, what they fear, and how the feared consequences of wishes may lead to behavioral

Figure 6.1 A model of therapeutic alliance

avoidances. Therapist and patient can carefully listen to configurations of wish, fear, and defensiveness occurring in the present moment and to put these configurations into words.

The therapist may be frequently asked for advice such as: "What should I do?" or "what would you do?" Therapists tactfully avoid direct answers in order to create space for the patient to form new appraisals and make their own choices. This clarifies the therapeutic alliance transactions, in showing that the patient has to maintain personal responsibility for choices. Nonetheless, the patient may continue to ask for direct guidance. In that case, it may be helpful to say something like, "I am concerned that, if I give you the advice you want, then you are relying perhaps too much on me to make your own personal choices . . . but if I don't give you the advice you specifically seek then you feel let down and uncertain about how to proceed. How should we understand this kind of situation?"

This kind of remark can focus the patient's attention and enhance their self-reflective awareness. Success in self-reflective awareness is a capacity developed over time that requires repetition in many sessions.

When a patient continues to ask for direct advice, the therapist can try other responses. For example, the therapist might say, "You are troubled on whether to stay with or leave your unsatisfactory boyfriend. You are asking me to help you arrive at a choice, and you even want me to make the decision for you. Perhaps you find it frustrating that I seem to just want to explore the matter further." The therapist is explaining the frustrations of the patient and defining for the patient the goals of therapy, which is to help the patient gain the capacities to make independent decisions, and the confidence in those skills.

An important aspect of such an approach is to ask the patient what he or she has heard the therapist say. In this example, a patient may reply, "You just don't care enough to help me but you can't come out and say that, so you say you are leaving the decision up to me." When you encourage the patient to listen and observe what they just said, the patient may become self-reflective. If so, the patient may be able to move forward and say, "Can we discuss the pros and cons of my options with my boyfriend, and why it isn't working well?"

Comparing and contrasting new and old relationship patterns

Personality growth represents the formation of new capacities for a variety of relationships. The patient learns these capacities by trying out new opportunities in new ways. The new ways develop new attitudes and schemas. The old ways tend to persist: the role-relationship models in the patient's repertoire at the start of therapy are not erased. They become dormant in terms of being checked from compulsive repetitions, and they are modified to match new capacities.

Clarification of a maladaptive relationship pattern assists the patient in learning to check automatic responses and tendencies toward specific actions. While the patient is learning new relationship models, insight can aid the process of acquiring new patterns. Insight is achieved by comparing the old pattern, raised to reflective self-awareness, with new ways of interpreting reality, with a focus on identifying misappraisals and dysfunctional beliefs.

Old patterns may have worked as the best available ways of coping with past situations. "Best available" means not necessarily the ideal action, but what the unique individual could think to do at the time. Broadening the available choices of action facilitates new self-narratives, helps the patient understand current re-enactments, and assists in planning when to check the habitual response system.

Conversations about relationship situations enable learning process of insight and change. Clarifying a pattern usually requires many examinations of stories about both real and fantasy situations with other people. At different times in this process, the therapist and patient can focus on present, past, and future situations.

For example, a patient was discussing a dispute with her mother that happened the day before the therapy session. Following the levels of formulation discussed in Chapter 1, the therapist clarified what happened in the episode memory. The patient developed feelings of anxiety right at the moment when her mother said she should cook every meal for her family rather than ordering take-out. Then the patient shifted into an angry state and disparaged her mother's mode of dress. While listening to the therapist's construction of this plausible sequence, the patient tried to take back what she had said about feeling hostile towards her mother.

Going deeper into the use of formulations, the therapist clarified that the patient tended to stifle the irritation caused by the mother's implied criticism. On a deeper level, the therapist was helping to clarify the relationship model in the present situation: was she an adult self in a squabble, or a child having an uproar at being criticized by her mother?

The therapist in this example was exploring a pattern in the current outside relationship between the patient and her mother, and looking at some possible roots of that current relationship pattern in the past. The patient might shift to feeling that the therapist was criticizing her, perhaps for "being childish." The patient may have felt insulted by the therapist remarking on her stifling her feelings of irritation. If so, the therapist might switch attention to the pattern as under enactment in the therapy situation itself.

The therapist could clarify that the intention of dealing with an avoidance maneuver was not to criticize it is occurring, but to explore what was happening in a way that promoted understanding the patient's reasons for potential anger. That is, the therapist may need to clarify a non-critical, learning-situation intention. This contrast between a critical role and a helper role builds the relationship experience of the deepening therapeutic alliance.

Once a working state in therapy was restored, the pattern of anger at criticism could then be clarified by examining how it developed in childhood. If unchecked, the pattern may continue. The therapist and patient together might then usually wonder what behaviors could replace it. How might the patient plan to react to such challenges to her self-esteem? The potential new action plan, of what to do when feeling insulted by a significant other, could be rehearsed in therapy.

For each period of time and each situation, the patient and therapist can explore emotional states, conflicts in exposing or stifling automatic emotional tendencies, and possible re-appraisals of new and old relationship patterns. Patterns are clarified by their replication across present, past, and anticipated future relationship situations, forming new narratives and promoting understanding. These general techniques are described in Table 6.1. In supervising training in exploratory psychotherapy, it may be helpful to use this table as a tool for discussion after clarifying a process in a therapy session presented by trainees. The goal in such a case is to identify effective techniques that achieve progressive change.

Narrating the middle ground: The difference between new and old patterns

As the therapeutic alliance deepens, the patient can differentiate more clearly between their habitual responses to desires, frustrations, and fears and new opportunities to re-define themselves and their relationships. Suppose the patient has a habitual pattern of suspicion that has been, at times, an obstacle in trusting others. This pattern could manifest as habitual suspicion of other's intentions, or dramatic feelings of impending abandonment during moments of friction or frustration that are actually ordinary relationship perturbations. With a minor intrusion on reality, such as a cancellation by the therapist, a maladaptive pattern of bitter emotional closing-off may be activated. The therapist helps the patient clarify their warded-off feelings and any distortions in beliefs about the therapist that these feelings represent. The transference beliefs are contrasted with the actual intentions and recent history within the present therapeutic relationship. Lower-functioning patients may benefit the most from such work to clarify transference feelings in contrast with therapeutic alliance attitudes such as trust and hope (Høglend, 2014).

Sample inquiries to clarify transference feelings include the following therapist remarks:

"Could we say you just blew up at me? I find myself wondering why."

"How do you imagine I might react to what you just said?"

Table 6.1 Some techniques for exploring maladaptive relationship patterns in different situations

Levels of attention	Present, past, and future relationship patterns			
	Present Era Social Situations	Present Moment Therapy Situation	Past Relationship Situations	Possible Future Relationship Situations
Patient's States of Mind	Identify interactions that lead to problematic states	Learn a self-reflective stance	Clarify whose states may have been imitated	Plan how to avoid triggers of under-modulated states
Conflicted Topics	Explore why emotional expressions are stifled or distorted	Counteract obstacles to disclosure	Examine sources of habits in coping and defending	Plan alternatives to habitual avoidance
Identity & Relationships	Stabilize rational views of self and other	Explore reasons for deflections from experiencing a trusting therapeutic alliance	Reappraise why maladaptive patterns developed	Encourage new action plans

As the patient clarifies the present feelings, his or her relation to past events may emerge. Subsequently, formulations may develop of the origins of a patient's core beliefs. Linkages to past memories and experiences enhances insight. Memories can be identified and new appraisals can occur that clarify how past coping strategies may not be suitable in the present.

Suppose a patient presents ambivalent transference feelings and says to the therapist, "I just don't feel like I am getting enough from you. Maybe you don't really care about that. You just sit there and plan to listen until your clock ticks to the end of the session. You get paid anyway . . . (falls silent and looks glum)."

The therapist's formulation of how the patient has an inaccurate dichotomous attitude of "you either love or hate me" enables the therapist to provide words to fit the patient's feelings in the present moment. Based on the formulations, the therapist can paraphrase the patient's words as: "You seem to be saying that since you feel I do not love you enough, I must be hating you behind a façade of professional concern. I understand that you are telling me you wished I cared more for you and that I seem only to be coldly professional. Does that seem to fit at all what you are telling me?" The patient may respond obscurely, "You are doing what you have been trained to do and no more." The therapist may answer, "I would be interested in knowing what 'more' would be."

Sometimes, alternatively, it may be useful to switch examination of a pattern in the therapy relationship to an outside relationship. The therapist could try, "You know, this moment between us reminds me of your dissatisfaction living with Ronald where you felt he didn't love you enough. You told me you felt like prodding him to hold you when he was working on his email, and he would not respond well, snapping at you for interrupting him. Perhaps you expect me to yell at you and hate you."

The patient may feel understood because the therapist remembers stories from previous sessions. The patient's distress may be reduced by the therapist's attention. In this example, the model of transactions is pertinent. The model starts with a wish, such as yearning for more warm attentiveness and empathy than is felt. The relative absence of what is desired leads the self to respond with a prod to get more gratifying attention. The other responds to the prod with irritation. Although Ronald reacted that way in the story, the therapist instead stayed with the patient, clarifying the maladaptive pattern and considering with the patient what else might happen. In this situation, the therapist is in the midst of a complex moment where, within the alliance, transference feelings are utilized to understand the maladaptive pattern more deeply.

As listed in Table 6.1, several techniques are being combined here to create an alternative narrative, during frustrating relationship moments, to prevent future repetitions of the scenario in which "Either you love me, or you hate me and I hate you." This dichotomous love-hate thinking in which there is no middle ground has created a maladaptive relationship pattern. Its repetition has been clarified by the following linkages: (1) what has happened in terms of the patient's emotional reaction in therapy, (2) in the ongoing situation between the patient and Ronald, and (3) how sullen prods may have worked in past situations, as with an inattentive and unkind parent (Bion, 1997; Ferro, 2011).

The therapy transactions are creating a narrative about a middle ground between extremes. If a therapeutic alliance is not allowing clarification of the here-and-now middle ground in the relationship with the therapist, the dichotomous love-or-hate pattern activated into transference feelings presents the therapist with a dilemma. The therapist anticipates that the patient will repeat the maladaptive pattern. The patient sees the situation with the therapist and with other relationships as having a polarity rather than a mature spectrum of possibilities. The patient experiences appropriate professional distance as if the self is being degraded. The patient must feel totally loved in order not to feel totally rejected.

Dilemmas can be formulated as situations in which the therapist experiences a "damned if you do and damned if you don't" choice between responses scripted by the patient. Once the nature of a dilemma is identified, the therapist may then attempt to clarify for the patient a middle zone that does not involve either extreme response. As that middle zone of safety is developed, the therapeutic alliance is deepened. The patient is encouraged to explore the dilemma that whatever the therapist does will be perceived negatively. As the patient understands and experiments with reflecting on middle-ground transactive possibilities with the therapist, a sign of progress may be observed, as the patient comes to change outside relationship transactions.

The therapist remains with the patient, calm in attitude, avoiding being provoked into any action that would remove attention from the topic of concern. If the patient finds the effort to look at both extremes of the dilemma confusing, the therapist may persist with very short, easily understood empathic statements. This hopefully creates a "holding environment" of the type described by Kohut (1977), Modell (1976), and Gedo and Goldberg (1975).

Gradually the patient will learn to transcend dichotomous thinking and will see the value of expanding the middle ground to allow an escape from the dilemma. As a consequence, the therapeutic alliance is enriched and the patient practices authentic discussions in a relationship.

Table 6.2 presents a sampling of ten such dilemmas.

Narrating stories in new ways

Patients can be encouraged to develop new insights into the behavior of others. When a patient describes a reaction of the other person in a relationship, the therapist can say, "Patients can be encouraged to develop new insights into the behavior of others." When a patient describes a reaction of the other person, "take a guess, what do you think she was probably thinking then?" This can expand a patient's perception of the other person's behavior and discourage the negative assumptions the patient may otherwise make out of habitual attitudes.

In anticipating how another person may respond to a request or overture made by the patient, several possibilities can be examined: dreaded responses, hoped-for responses, and realistic "in-between" responses. Both therapist and patient can

Table 6.2 Ten sample dilemmas

1	a)	The patient is frightened of inability to structure and communicate inner experiences and control chaotic thoughts and emotions.
	b)	But if the therapist attempts to structure the communication of these ideas and feelings, the patient views this attempt as an invasion and fear domination.
2	a)	The patient manifests helplessness and dependency upon the therapist for guidance.
	b)	But if the therapist addresses this attitude or indicates the necessity for assuming personal responsibility, the patient feels so neglected or overwhelmed by demands that apathetic withdrawal follows.
3	a)	The patient is so deflated and demoralized that very little impetus to engage in work is present.
	b)	But if the therapist addresses this attitude or encourages the patient to a more positive view, then the patient perceives the therapist is too unempathic and unrealistically optimistic and feels increasingly hopeless.
4	a)	The patient feels entitled to more than the therapist can give and so feels neglected and hostile.
	b)	But if the therapist is always flexible and makes any appointment times or phone calls and email exchanges that the patient requests then the patient feels too special to have to work in therapy.
5	a)	The patient exhibits a tendency to act out.
	b)	But if the therapist interprets this tendency as maladaptive and needing increased control, the patient views that interpretation as criticism and becomes increasingly rebellious.
6	a)	The patient does little besides repetitively express personal suffering.
	b)	But if the therapist addresses this pattern and encourages other work, the patient feels so misunderstood that only increased expressions of suffering or withdrawal will take place.
7	a)	The patient is so passive that all initiative is placed with the therapist.
	b)	But if the therapist becomes active in fostering communication, the patient complies blandly without processing meanings personally.
8	a)	The patient is preoccupied with challenging the therapist to show competency and strength.
	b)	But if the therapist addresses this challenge by reassuring the patient about having sufficient expertise, the patient either obstinately increases the challenge or submits obsequiously and inauthentically.
9	a)	The patient presents in a contrived and inauthentic manner in which substitute emotions are used to hide what the therapist infers may be authentic ones.
	b)	But if the therapist confronts the contrived affect, the patient becomes confused.
10	a)	The patient does not express certain ideas and feelings central to core aspects of important topics.
	b)	But if the therapist addresses this avoidance, the patient experiences the therapists confrontation as corrosively scornful.

examine this middle ground together. Such techniques can increase a patient's emotional intelligence and positively affect the patient's life. As mentioned, the patient may begin to show more patience and concern in conversations with others.

The middle ground also allows an adult reconsideration of childhood experiences, in which parents may be seen as less dichotomous and more complex in their own needs and actions. Some degree of forgiveness or at least understanding may occur, and that can strengthen the patient's own self-narrative and sense of identity.

Summary

Patients can improve their capacity to have satisfying relationships through new experiences in the relationship with the therapist. Attitudes can be clarified and interpreted as they occurred in the past, as they occur now in therapy, and as they may occur in relationships outside of therapy. The therapeutic alliance enhances the possibilities for new, more harmonious relationship experiences.

7

Improving maladaptive patterns in sexual relationships

Sexual relationships are complex for a number of reasons, including cultural variations in social norms and taboos. Given that explicit sexual stories may be emotionally difficult to tell in therapy, patterns are often harder to clarify. As a result, the patient's sexuality may be treated as a radioactive topic to be quarantined under a lead shield. An enriched therapeutic alliance makes the shield unnecessary and patterns may be observed, formulated, and handled with safe techniques.

Observation

Gender and sexual preferences form an important part of identity and self-presentations. The patient may display conflicting signs in how they seem to want the therapist to regard them as having certain gender characteristics, or to find them physically attractive. The therapist can observe his or her own comfort and discomfort, which may indicate early signs of such conflicts within the patient.

As trust and rapport develop, the patient may begin to tell the stories of their relationships, giving an opportunity for the therapist to observe where the patient reports problems or becomes uncomfortable and avoidant. In most cases, investigating maladaptive sexual relationship patterns occurs later in the therapy period. Then reports may be elaborated, and the therapist can better observe when acute discomfort occurs.

Sexual practices involve a variety of physical connections, with possibilities that range from cooperation and equality to roles of relative domination/assertiveness and passivity/subordination. This range of practices may or may not be reported as problematic by the patient, in which they complain that either the self or other feels non-participatory, or at the other extreme, that one partner may excessively and aggressively control the other.

States that the patient may report include distress, dissatisfaction, and difficulty achieving orgasm. Empathy, compassion, and kindness can be lost during sexual relations. Sexuality can also be blunted by remoteness rather than sharing, or infused with hostility. Blame and accusation can destroy a couple's sexual connection and shatter relationships.

Formulation

The clinician formulates relationship patterns using the elements of self attributes, attributes of the other, and what is expected as a map of possible or intended interactions. That means what the patient may offer or request, how the other person responds, and how the self reacts to both what the other has or has not done, and how the self had behaved. Sexual desire, which plays a key role in relationship patterns, is an important element but the patterns of its play or inhibition may be late additions to understanding repetitive patterns that may need to change.

The individual's desire is often formed in relation to certain characteristics of the other's appearance and activities. These characteristics come from a complex matrix of beliefs arising from biological, social, and developmental experiences. To make matters even more complex, the high emotionality of sex and gender means that desire may be associated with feared consequences. Unraveling this complexity requires gradual formulations.

Familiarity with general developmental psychology patterns can help the therapist frame the issues for the individual patient being treated. The most troublesome sexual attitudes that persist into adulthood are rooted in childhood sexual abuse because desire can be confused with fear of sexual predation and even with unconscious efforts to master predation by repetition of circumstances (Stoller, 1968; Stolorow & Lachmann, 1980; J. Herman, 2000). The effects of childhood sexual abuse may cause a child to move towards adolescent development with confusion about sexuality, extreme inhibition, or excessive boldness. The first sexual experiences of an immature self also lead to role-relationship models that can organize maladaptive patterns that persist into middle adulthood.

The therapist seeks to formulate why distress or defenses interfere with the patient's expressed or avoided aims at pleasure and closeness. Attitudes are harder to express than feeling states, and formulation aims at clarifying patterns. Wishes connected to feared consequences may lead to defensive inhibitions that can prevent deep relationships. Questions to consider include: How does the patient present desires and prohibitions in social life? As already mentioned, what are the expected positive and negative responses of the other? How does the self judge what happens, that is, on reappraisal does the self as critic see the self as actor as portraying good or bad self-attributes? Does the patient tend to expect approval or disapproval in the larger social sphere? It is also important to formulate any dilemmas the therapist faces because the patient's desires may be carried into transference re-enactments.

Childhood sexual abuse is common and can result in a role-relationship model in which the self is seen as weak, vulnerable, or violated, while the other is seen as an overpowering master or even a predator (Briere and Elliot, 2003). When the abuse is by a parent that the child loves, the young mind faces a difficult problem. For example, a child may develop a role-relationship model in which father is a selfish molester, who traumatizes her as a helpless victim.

At the same time, the child may also see father as a kind protector, who loves as a parent should. The father in this situation is sometimes a good parent and sometimes a terrifying one. His self-state variation fosters contradictory self-states in the child and a tendency towards dissociation during relationship experiences that are similar in contexts.

Likewise, the perpetrator can be a mother, uncle, aunt, older sibling, religious leader, sports coach, and other authority figures. Proper formulation may reconstruct the repertoire of relevant role-relationship models that the child carried forward into adult attitude structures.

Some sexual violations are not traumatic for the child at the time that the actions take place. The child may enjoy what they are told is fond attention and even find the sexual advances pleasurable. He or she can mistakenly view the abuser as a loved and loving figure. Only later does the child realize, perhaps then with great rage, that the abuser was actually a selfish aggressor. A state of horror may ensue when a person realizes, perhaps months or even years later, that there was a violation of early trust.

Such instances become *retrospective traumas*. In hindsight, an individual may realize that the abusive figure was irresponsibly and reprehensibly harmful. This can form a devastating sense of grievance and cause the abused victim to form revenge fantasies at a conscious or an unconscious level. Unlocking these unconscious attitudes may help the victim reappraise and re-narrate the whole story and realize that these past experiences may relate to current re-enactments.

These child sexual abuse schemas may involve more than a dyad between victim and aggressor: a third party may be involved. For example, if a father sexually abuses his daughter and the mother does not step in to protect the girl, the child may view the mother as failing to be an adequate caretaker. In such cases, attitudes of grievance can imbue both parents.

Childhood sexual trauma has at least three possible lasting consequences: the child assimilates the victim role and repeats the role as an adult; the child learns the reciprocal aggressor role through identification and enacts it later in life; or the child is unable to reconcile the extremely different roles of caretaker and abuser in one individual. This last possible scenario may impair the child's self-organization and his or her ability to love and trust another person in a loving sexual relationship.

Children who are emotionally, physically, or sexually abused sometimes come to believe—either because they have been taught it or because they assume it—that their innate "badness" has caused their terrible circumstances. Sometimes a child is faulted for simply having asked for his or her own needs to be met. From then on, that child may have difficulty expressing his or her wishes. A child may even feel unworthy to live out a heartfelt dream.

Another pattern is to defend the self by taking the strong role of the aggressor in sexual transactions. In identification with the aggressor, the child may emerge as an adult who must struggle to control aggressive impulses. Such hostile components may include anger misplaced into the present for being a victim in the past. The patient with such a pattern in adulthood may be seeking satisfaction by subjugating, degrading, or even injuring another person. Part of the gratification may come from exerting power over the degraded other.

For some people, abusive role-relationship models become part of a search for sexual excitement: they use the thrill of their aggression, as well as the fear instilled in the other, to overcome a lack of erotic excitement that they associate with ordinary sexual practices. Such dynamics may occur in patterns of voyeurism or exhibitionism, which can involve elements of hostility. In voyeurism the other is forced to be seen by the self; viewing another person against his or her will is a form of aggression upon the victim. Exposing the self to show off and solicit interest is another normal component of sexuality that can be exaggerated due to one's limitations in arousal. A person might exhibit him or herself in a variety of ways, enjoying the belief that the person who sees them, who is forced to look, has become their victim.

Childhood sexual abuse can also reinforce any inherent dispositions toward self-degradation. The submissive role involves the expectation of satisfaction by allowing a powerful partner to tie them up, use handcuffs, or otherwise forcibly subjugate them. At times, vulnerability is part of a non-verbal attitude that says in effect, "I am not responsible for submitting to the pleasures that I am about to experience." When carried beyond cooperative play, such fantasies can destroy tenderness and true caring. However, new, non-submissive erotic attitudes can be learned by repeated conscious reflection, social support, and new experiences of mutuality.

Recent adult episodes may have led to phobic reactions to sexuality. For example, a young woman in her twenties came in for brief therapy after her first attempt at intercourse had an unfortunate result because of the ineptitude of her boyfriend. He failed to consummate the experience and rather than share his frustration he told her she disgusted him because she had "a very bad vagina." She had an accurate hunch that he was escaping from embarrassment in a selfish way but she still felt overwhelmed by his harsh reaction of blaming and depreciating her. Clarification improved her courage and body image in a relatively rapid way, which might have not been the case without her secure childhood background.

Technique

The therapist enhances observations by asking questions about sexuality including frequency, satisfaction, longing, and fantasies. Without the existence of a strong therapeutic alliance, details about sexual practices, masturbation fantasies, and sexual daydreams are unlikely to be revealed. As the relevant topics are presented as problems by the patient, more details about patterns can be obtained. This usually involves helping the patient focus on difficult areas by asking questions. The questions may also in and of themselves have a psycho educational component.

The therapist should ask about emerging fears before or during erotic moments. The therapist can inquire about feelings of shame to clarify the patient's conflicted values. Such questioning may reveal areas of conspicuous ignorance about sexual practices, as well as provide an opportunity for psycho education. Usually, however, progress will be made by gradual clarification and interpretation of maladaptive patterns. By paying attention over time, guided in part by questions raised by the therapist, patient can learn how to describe a shift in self-states that occur during sexuality.

The following examples of Amber and Richard illustrate paths to growth that involve an increased use of reasoned thinking to solidify a sense of identity and enrich the sexual components of relationships. By practicing self-awareness and self-conscious thought, they were both able to increase self-regulation in regard to emergent sexual motivations. The first example is of an erotic transference and relates to the previous chapter on deepening a therapeutic alliance by using transference enactments to achieve personality growth in the patient.

A patient may use erotic transference reactions, and flirtatious behavior leading to erotic counter-transference, as tests to see if the therapist will be a strong caring figure who remains a trustworthy ally. Although the patient may appear to be asking for erotic attention, in such scenarios the patient may not want a sexual encounter. Instead the patient has an unconscious aim to find a figure who is capable of resisting a sexual re-enactment and who instead practices appropriate restraint and compassionate care.

Amber: Erotic transference re-enactment

Amber, a 34-year-old single health professional, met the diagnostic criteria for both Major Depressive Disorder and Histrionic Personality Disorder. Her initial symptoms had been partially ameliorated with an anti-depressant medication. In psychotherapy, support and psycho education had been helpful. At the present phase of her treatment she had been reviewing a pattern of frequent relationship ruptures and her reactive medley of sorrow, fear, shame, and anger states.

Her maladaptive relationship cycles typically began in a state of loneliness, leading to an imperative search for someone to appease her longing to be loved. She would quickly fall in love with anyone who showed her a lot of attention. All too soon, she felt sexually used, deserted, and angry. The desperate loneliness that followed would restart the cycle, as she impulsively latched onto the next man who demonstrated interest in her.

Amber had provided the therapist a history full of the resentment and bitterness that she felt toward her uncle for abusing her when she was 15 years of age. At the time of this abuse, she did not feel mistreated. Instead, she felt that the sexual encounter was a consensual one of romantic true love and shared erotic pleasure. Yet, two years later, at the age of 17, she came to view this episode in retrospect as a betrayal of her trust. From that time on, she carried a grievance against her uncle because he had abused her.

Amber entered adulthood with a sense of longing for a love that could solidify her sense of identity. By the age of 30, she recognized that she had repeatedly re-enacted unsatisfying sexual relationships with men, which were destructive to

Figure 7.1 Early phase of Amber's maladaptive pattern

her wellbeing rather than being self-reparative. Demoralization after the last relationship rupture fed into a first episode of clinical depression, and she felt that her life would continue to be a "life of sorrows." At 34, she felt desperate for "a happy life," which she defined as marriage and children. It was not enough that she was successful and secure in her profession.

In one session, in a middle phase of therapy, she displayed her body erotically and told her therapist she loved him. Quite insistently she stood up and said, "Hold me! I need you to show me that you care. That will make me feel that life is worth living! Otherwise, who knows what I will do?" The scenario that she consciously believed she was enacting is formulated in the form of the role-relationship model in Figure 7.1. The therapist did not reciprocate the roles depicted in Figure 7.1, and instead asked her to sit down so they could talk this over.

Amber sat down looking distressed. The therapist said, "Please let it be enough that I understand the longing for love that you are feeling. Can you tolerate your distress and longing for a while? I want to talk it over with you, without hugging." The therapist maintained a calm demeanor. Amber then cried and expressed feelings of being rejected. The therapist said, "It is a good sign that you can put this into words." Amber had been in an under-modulated state. She then shifted into a more controlled working state, in which she understood what was going on and could process ideas – hers and the therapist's – in an ongoing emotional conversation. This episode was examined in serial sessions.

In those sessions, the therapist and Amber used verbal labels to clarify the respective roles of self and other as they were enacted in stories about her important previous sexual relationships. Through these discussions her hopes were clarified and interpreted in relation to the new current narratives of her past experiences. The desired role-relationship model depicted in Figure 7.1 was clarified, including her usual maladaptive transformation into the dreaded pattern of rejection and desperate loneliness. The end story of the pattern of relationship ruptures is depicted in Figure 7.2.

As Amber re-enacted her core attitude in a series of transference states and therapeutic alliance states, the therapist's responses led to progress in further clarifying the roles in their deepening therapeutic alliance. Her trust gradually increased with the therapist's continued non-critical responses that promoted

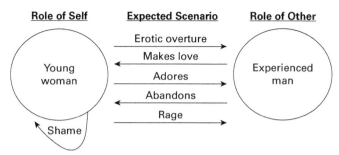

Figure 7.2 Later phase of Amber's maladaptive pattern

Figure 7.3 Roles of a relationship in a therapeutic alliance

insight and conversation. She expressed sadness as she reconsidered her narrative about her childhood abuse from a stance of reflective self-awareness.

The consistency and enriched realization of the therapeutic alliance was an important corrective relationship experience. In the new relationship experience, the therapist showed his value of caring for her as a person and his interest in her personality growth. The frame was clear: there would never be engagement of a sexual relationship. The therapeutic alliance as experienced by Amber is shown in Figure 7.3

For a therapist to enable a patient to learn from new experiences, he or she needs to be aware of and avoid two technical errors. As discussed earlier in by Table 6.2 as a dilemma: the therapist should not be so warm as to indicate a possible boundary crossing, and the therapist should not be so cold as to appear remote, which can be misinterpreted by the patient as being totally rejecting. In Amber's case, the therapist maintained eye contact to avoid appearing remote and did not offer to reciprocate a hug.

As with Amber, a therapist may respond to seductive behaviors by setting appropriate boundaries defining the limits of the relationship, while emphasizing mutual trust-building and verbal communication. The patient may react angrily at first if they feel rejected. However, the patient will eventually recognize that what is occurring in therapy is not rejection. Instead, it is a compassionate and

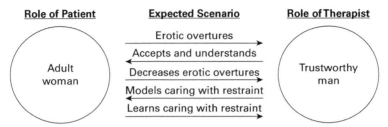

Figure 7.4 Learning from the evolving therapeutic alliance

restrained form of continuous caring, as shown in Figure 7.4. Figure 7.4 shows the new role-relationship model of the therapeutic alliance as eventually experienced by Amber. The process was helped along by verbal clarifications and appraisals. Some of the therapist's intended actions and statements to Amber are illustrated in Table 7.1.

Richard

Curbing certain sexual activities may require moral restraint. The impulses to engage in habitual pleasures may need to be controlled in order for the individual to learn new relationship patterns that resonate with traditional values. The case of Richard illustrates how implicit rules of erotic behavior can be altered by discussing and thinking about them explicitly.

Richard was a young, rich, handsome, and bright lawyer who nonetheless was chronically bitter. He would repeatedly become sexually attracted to a woman attached to another man, usually an acquaintance or a friend. He would be quite charming to the woman and initially feel thrilled by her interest. When possible, he quickly persuaded her to have sex. Both in the context of a flirtation or an affair, his erotic states were transient, and he would quickly lose interest in the woman. When the relationship ended, he would feel bitter as if it were her fault. He felt indifferent towards single women who signaled that they might be available and interested in him.

Richard described a scenario with a new woman, Anne, who was romantically and sexually involved with his friend Bob. When he was alone with her one night, he had an impulse to ask Anne to let him give her a massage, hoping that it would become erotic. He realized such an affair would interfere with both Anne's and his relationship with Bob. He restrained the impulse because he thought he would have to tell his therapist if he repeated his habitual scenario. Having restrained himself, he expected approval from the therapist.

Richard said, "So, that's what didn't happen (and fell silent)."

The therapist said, "I think some kind of value judgment is in the air."

Richard replied, "What?! You don't approve?!"

The therapist explained, "You know that I am supportive of your efforts to change your patterns, and this episode looks like a gain in self-governance.

Table 7.1 Therapeutic actions

Therapeutic action	Sample statement
Expressing empathy	*"I understand from what you are saying that you are feeling angry at me because you want us to express affection for one another."*
Clarifying the framework of therapeutic alliance	*"You want us to express physical affection for one another, but I cannot reciprocate."*
Interpretation of the transference	*"Because I decline to hug, I think that you mistakenly experience my adhering to my mission to clarify with you what is happening as a cold and unfeeling rejection of your feelings."*
Interpretation of the therapeutic alliance	*"You mistakenly experience me as cold and rejecting, yet I am acting on your behalf."*
Clarifying professional boundaries	*"My job is being your therapist and helping you safely tell me your thoughts and feelings."*
Expression of non-critical positive regard	*"My aim is not to relieve you of these yearnings, but rather, to help you stop repeating a cycle that leads to states of blame, anger, sadness, and self-disgust."*
Interpretation of the therapeutic alliance and contrasting interpretation of transference	*"I am not coldly rejecting you, although I know that you feel like that is happening."*
Expression of shared values for therapy	*"I care about your future."*
Teaching governance of impulses	*"I hope you can learn to love others in the future by using restraint until it is safe for you to be fully spontaneous."*
Summary of new relationship scenario	*"Increasing your capacities for tolerating this pain can bring you to a state of readiness to both love and be loved with a sense of enduring commitment, rather than having a short romance that ends in grievance and feelings of self-disgust."*
Negotiating and reaffirming therapeutic goals	*"I am asking you to fully express to me your feelings, and to regard restraint as a commitment to honor opportunities that you can make possible in your future."*

What I am asking is, how might you put your own self-appraisals and values into words?"

The conversation continued for a long time. Richard wanted praise from the therapist, who wanted to focus on Richard's own self-appraisal. Eventually Richard responded in a way that can be paraphrased as follows: "If I had sex with Anne, the consequences would have been that I would have harmed both her and Bob. I want to stop repeating this pattern. I will restrain myself. I will feel sexually frustrated and bored; however, retaining my pride and self-approval is more important to me than the frustration. I can satisfy my desires in some other way, later, with better, and more thoughtful choices of an intimate partner." This summarized what Richard thought that the therapist wanted to hear. Nonetheless, his verbal explanation enhanced Richard's value prioritizations and contributed to enhanced self-coherence in the organization of his identity, as discussed in Chapter 2 (Horowitz, 2009, 2014). He gradually could take responsibility for heightened self-governance.

Working on this relationship pattern led Richard to expand on another value of his: to fulfill a goal of being a mighty man. He thought that a bold, strong man was entitled to have sex with many women. His father, whom he regarded as such a man, had many flagrant affairs without apparent deleterious consequences.

Now, in a new narrative, Richard thought his father used sexual thrill seeking in part as a way out of his brooding. Richard was repeating that pattern. This kind of work in therapy led to conversions about an emergent transference feeling. A tentative formulation was that Richard unconsciously felt guilty about hurting the women that he seduced and abandoned, while consciously he felt criticism stemming from others like his friend Bob or the therapist.

During a period of negative transference, Richard had a fantasy of taking revenge on the therapist for disapproving of his actions by seducing the therapist's wife. As a child, Richard wanted constant gratification of his appetites and expected his parents to make this happen. While he frequently got his way, when he did not, he felt bitter. This established an attitude that Richard should come first, and people who did not place him as their highest priority deserved a righteous punishment. This primitive and implicit value, unstated in words until it became explicit in the dialogue that took place in therapy, justified him in avoiding his own moral sense that his actions were unethical.

In other words, during childhood Richard had etched in a primitive and inarticulate value, which when put into words, was akin to the following: "Selfish parents should receive a righteous punishment for depriving a child of love and care. Now my so-called therapist is just like them." Richard and the therapist clarified, interpreted, and modified this attitude to a more insightful stance: "I accept that my parents looked after their own interests, and were not always attentive enough to me." He could also describe the therapeutic alliance: "I guess you are helping me look after myself in a better way than I have done."

Repetition of this new conscious value, which contrasted with his primitive, only self-serving value, built a stronger sense of self-command, empathy for himself as a child, and regard for his parents as imperfect humans. This work further strengthened the therapeutic alliance and clarified future goals in Richard's conscious mind.

Any regression toward the enactment of some kind of revenge fantasy was held in check by his consciously developed principles, which now included being consistent in his responsibilities to care for himself and others (Holmes, 2011). In addition, his increased reflective awareness in the context of a new narrative with mature empathy for his parents led him to reconnect with them. This included forgiveness for his unconscious past grievances and alleviation of his unconscious guilt for his revenge fantasies (Kealy and Ogrodnikzuk, 2014; Smith, 2008). Sexual domination was no longer a form of power and manipulation.

Richard felt optimistic that he could pursue continuity and constancy in loving relationships. He began to wonder what he would be like as a father, a new narrative of his future goals.

Summary

Sexuality is a complex feature of personality that is strongly linked to gender identifications, relationship models, and both personal and cultural values. Transference feelings may change as they arise from complex configurations developed in the past. Psychotherapy never includes a sexual relationship between patient and therapist. Advances in such relationship capacities are to be gained by the patient imagining and then having new kinds of experiences outside of therapy. In therapy, the patient's memories, fantasies, and imagined future are explored, and transference feelings contained and changed in the apt development of therapeutic alliance role-relationship models.

Control and emotional regulation

This section on emotional regulation has three chapters. The first chapter (8) expands on theory about how and why potential emotions are controlled. The next chapter (9) focuses on observing, formulating, and using techniques to counteract defense mechanisms: habitual operations that may be found in reviewing stories that a patient tells about past life. The third chapter (10) focuses on very immediate observations, those that can be made on the spot in therapy, leading to formulation of techniques of immediate intervention that can teach a patient capacities for new modes of control that permit fuller emotional experiencing.

8

Control of unconscious emotional potentials

Preconscious information processing includes control of what ideas are promoted to conscious representation. Ideas associated with emotional threats of the kind that would otherwise lead into dreaded states of mind can be inhibited or distorted. Nonetheless, activated memories, activated unconscious fantasies, sensory perceptions, and preconscious thought can all arouse emotion. The combination of emotional arousal and ideational inhibitions can lead to mysterious moods and emotions that remain unlabeled with words. Therapists can formulate possible reasons for the mysterious mood or unverbalized affect, and use attention-focusing techniques to help the patient understand what is going on, including the danger being avoided by defensiveness.

Observation

The therapist notes shifts in the patient that seem to avoid emotional expression. The topic at the point of the observed shift is registered. This is a topic worthy of safe exploration to both reach a decision point and to help the patient increase emotional tolerance.

For example, a patient may have sorrow from the death of a parent that in the past was too dangerous to experience. Now, the patient may feel safe enough to emotionally thaw out the frozen grief. Memories may be activated. In a therapeutic alliance the sorrow seems tolerable, so the suppressed memories can reach awareness and be discussed. At this point, a formerly incomplete mourning process can move forward and richer narrative about the meanings of the loss to the self can be achieved. In the midst of such work, however, it is common for the patient to repeatedly avoid certain emotional themes.

Even if patients consciously intend to remember a serious life event, they may be observed in the moment to inhibit activation of a particular emergent memory. For example, after the death of a loved wife, a husband may want to recall her face looking affectionately upon him, but he finds that the image will not come into visual representation in the mind's eye. The discrepancy between the desired closeness to the lost wife and the actuality of her permanent absence would be overwhelming. In the future, after a period of mourning has made the memory of his wife safer to contemplate, the images will more readily come to the surface of conscious thought. The information is not lost, but rather, at the moment, it is observed by the therapist to be avoided unconsciously in spite of conscious intentions to represent it.

What the patient wanted to think about, and theoretically could think about, did not appear. Similarly, with the same patient, at a different time, one might observe experiences of intrusive, unbidden images of the wife's face. These observations indicate preconscious regulatory process are operating: inhibiting or insisting upon the conscious visual images of the face. These deflections from ordinary conscious attention control indicate conflict and incomplete topical processing.

Formulation

In some phases of response to stress, such as in the example of the loss of a loved one, patients may deflect from ordinary control of emotion to enter a state of over-control, as in periods of denial and numbing, or under-control, as in periods of unbidden ideas and feeling flooded with intense negative emotions such as yearning and heart-sickness. As the stress response is completed, emotional control returns from these extremes to a middle range, with neither under- nor over-control, even when experiencing distressing feelings such a sadness.

In such instances the formulation may focus on inferring where the patient is in a process of working through a difficult topic. Such formulations can be psycho-educational and supportive when shared with the patient: they give an idea about a progress moving forward rather than enduring always in the present level of suffering (Horowitz, 2011). Formulating what phase the patient is in may lead to techniques for that degree of emotional regulation: helping with containment in under-modulated states, and with reducing avoidance in over-modulated states.

One way to formulate the dynamic between potential emotional experiences and efforts to control them is to consider a matching process. Current appraisals of perceived situations are matched with enduring schematizations. Mismatches lead to emotional responses which in a basic way are motivations to plan actions so as to make a match occur. The emotions allow the patient and therapist to examine discrepancies between past hopes and future expectations.

Understanding how a mismatch generates emotion leads to a greater sense of control in the patient, even if the feelings experienced by the patient are unpleasant ones. In working states, the experience of fear, rage, and sadness motivates coping efforts. Such formulations lead to efforts to focus attention on problems that need to be solved. Progress can occur as calmer mental states are stabilized, in a kind of step-by-step approach.

Unintegrated memories of trauma or loss will continue to persist as active memories and intrusive fantasies or bad dreams until a new narrative integrates current self with past self. These incompletely processed themes leave partially unanswered questions of what the trauma and/or loss means for the future. Formulation of such questions leads to focused attention in treatment. Eventually, the root question is: how may self and future expectations be modified to fit realistic probabilities for a better life? The therapist plans to use techniques that keep the focus while allowing dose-by-conceptualizations that keep emotional arousals within the tolerable limits usually necessary for clear thinking and discussion.

Formulations involve configurations that progressively identify a network of linked associations. Configurations connect elements of memory, including earlier perceptions and memories of self-states with high emotional alarm, pain, or distress, with a readiness to react instantly to danger. Some previously established connections between idea and affective arousal are not rational in the present moment: for example, the smell of smoke, though harmless, can lead to an anxiety attack in a patient because that smell occurred during a terrifying fire long ago.

Patients with early conditioned associations can encounter a reminder of a past trauma and react with feelings that are unclear. They do not know why the felt state of experience and fragmentary images came to their mind. Both insight-promoting and exposure techniques can be used, once the formulation is made, to decondition the associational connection. Making the implicit and procedural memories explicit and declarative are part of this adaptive change.

Susan: Linking associations and sharing formulations

Susan had a panic attack in an elevator on the way to a psychotherapy session. During the session, the conversation examined the moment triggering the fear: a person in the elevator who had an odor that gave her a sudden headache followed by feelings of impending doom. The odor resembled the smell of alcohol on the breath of an uncle who raped her as an adolescent. Susan could realize why the odor triggered the headache as the association was made to the memory.

The therapist guessed that the work so far in therapy had made it safer to remember the adolescent trauma. Some aspects of memory are "active," even if these memories are also inhibited, in that they are marked for later conscious processing. A traumatic experience such as the rape of Susan may reside in this category of active memory, and intrusively return later for further processing of meaning. This intrusive pattern continues until the memory has been sufficiently reviewed and articulated by self-organizing narratives. In Susan's case she was ready to not only have the fear reaction to the odor, but to connect it to the past. In such cases, the patient does not want to know what happened, or further, what might happen emotionally if a locked away memory or fantasy is revived. The inhibitory processes are defensive as they serve the mind's wish to avoid entering into intensely emotional and dreaded states (Olson et al., 2011: Rice and Hoffman, 2014).

Technique

Although the therapist cannot know precisely what is warded off, observing the consequences of under- or over-control helps the therapist to arrive at tentative formulations. These formulations are intentionally shared with the patient.

Table 8.1 Patient activities involving awareness, insight, and decision-making

	Awareness	Insight	Decision-Making
Self-States	Knowing when a change in mood occurs	Understanding how and why a change in mood occurs	Planning how to avoid entry into under-modulated states
Changing Control of Emotions	Recognizing avoidance	Realizing how and why the avoidance occurs	Choosing to focus attention on, and rework, the avoided topic
Attitudes	Learning about new qualities of self and relationships	Understanding the differences between old and new concepts of self, and that the self can now tolerate emotions	Choosing and rehearsing new roles and activities

The aim is joint understanding as well as the patient learning to tolerate and express emotion.

Explanatory understanding at the surface level enhances the patient observing the consequences of under- or over-control at deeper level, the method promotes insight into how the maladaptive behavior developed. Then, looking towards the future, the therapist and patient explore new choices that can lead to more harmonious patterns. An overview of techniques to promote explanatory understanding is found in Table 8.1.

The examples of technique that follow involve stressful events that delivered bad news about the person's hoped-for identity roles. Shame is hard to bear and warding off that potential emotion motivated both Steve and Amy to exercise avoidance maneuvers that had to be modified in order to arrive at better coping strategies. Consciousness is an excellent tool for solving difficult problems, as long as the problems and associated ideas are clearly identified.

Steve: Avoidance of shame

Steve was a surgical resident at a crucial level of training that would dictate his future career. During this training, the faculty surgeon with whom he worked told Steve that, in spite of Steve's diligent efforts at practicing the necessary techniques, he was not meeting the required standards of skill in performing surgeries. In addition, the faculty surgeon stated that even with more practice, Steve seemed unlikely to acquire the fine motor skills required. Of course, this feedback was very bad news for the resident. For years, Steve had wanted to become a great surgeon. He felt deeply depressed and sought psychotherapy

The discrepancy between the new information, that he had mediocre skills in key areas, and Steve's understanding that he needed great surgical skills to succeed, threatened to bring on a painful emotional realization that he was likely to fail as a surgeon. This became a central topic for attention. On formulation it seemed that his mind unconsciously anticipated the danger of entering a dreaded state of mind: the intense feelings of shame that would accompany the admission of his failure to achieve a long-held goal. He inhibited some lines of thought to avoid this shameful state of mind.

A defensive stance kept him from realizing the full implications of the faculty surgeon's remarks, namely, that Steve should consider a move to another related medical fellowship for advanced training. The therapist asked for more details on this subtopic. Steve noticeably avoided this topic, just as he had selectively ignored the suggestions and feedback from his mentor, unconsciously choosing not to reflect on their meanings with this therapist. Instead Steve belittled the opinions of the faculty surgeon.

Steve's maladaptive avoidance strategies of making others rather than himself the target of criticism were defensive compromises. His mood was stabilized at a tolerably positive level, but at the expense of not assimilating useful information about the reality of his professional skills. The reality was that, in his mentor's opinion, even if he continued to practice and develop his surgical skills, he might not progress well in this specific specialty.

The therapist suggested to Steve that he was not exploring this important topic in the timely manner that career choices might require. Steve criticized the therapist. The therapist said he did not feel belittled by Steve's critique of what he said and he would not belittle Steve for what Steve had to say.

This challenge reinforced the therapeutic alliance instead of Steve's self-defense mechanism. By thinking carefully, in the safe context of a therapeutic alliance, Steve did set aside his defensive stance, tolerate his distress, and worked with the therapist to make a reasoned choice on the basis of probabilities and possibilities. Steve decided that he could choose to practice dexterities in new ways, and see how the faculty would respond with encouragement or discouragement. He could choose if and how to exit from his current track gracefully and begin to pursue another specialty that would utilize his other, stronger abilities, for example, his ability to make excellent diagnostic assessments.

To make apt choices, Steve had to tolerate the unpleasant emotions involved in processing the information he had available. He needed, with the help of conversations with the therapist, to examine possibilities from a standpoint of assessing himself as an adult with real capacities and with the requisite courage to reach a conclusion of what to do next. And to do well, he would need to avoid entry into self-states organized by regressive, bad, weak, or unworthy self-schemas. These degraded self-images would generate too much shame. The therapist continued to repeat Steve's reports of events that activated Steve's realistic beliefs around his self-efficacy. These repetitions kept the reactive shame emotion within tolerable limits for realistic thinking and planning.

The therapist was active in focusing attention, helping Steve review in tolerable doses the shame-evolving memory and its implications on his previous goals. If Steve had all at once contemplated the full range of potentially catastrophic consequences of the negative feedback from his supervisor, it would have been an emotional avalanche. For example, it could have brought on contemplations of his father's potential condemnation of his failure, his shame in front of friends, his potentially disastrous career future, and memories of a variety of experiences of incompetence experienced while he was in grade school. His stance of defensive coping through avoidance would have crumbled, and he would have been devastated by an uncontrollable storm of intense emotion. In contrast, tolerable doses of information and emotion helped Steve to develop a new self-narrative.

A patient like Steve may feel powerful because of activation of a self-schema as inordinately strong. That can be fueled by seizing the critic role, such as Steve's transference defense of belittling the therapist. At other times, Steve felt fragile and vulnerable because of activation of a self-schema as inordinately weak. Neither of the two extreme views was an accurate account of the self and, as in Amy's case, finding a middle ground between strong and vulnerable traits helped in creating a gradual and hopeful self-narrative for the future.

The next example also involved unexpected bad news that affected her future and her current sense of identity. The potential for shame led to intrusive painful feeling that the patient attempted to avoid.

Amy: Extreme trains of thought

Amy anticipated a promotion, with a hefty increase in salary and new leadership duties in her department. She was clearly in the line for this position because she was well respected by both her superiors and those whom she supervised. However, the economic collapse of the global market for the organization's products deeply affected her company. The entire sector where she worked was suddenly closed and the relevant part of the business was sold to another corporation.

This serious life event occurred in the midst of therapy that had been focused on identity and relationship problems for a year, with excellent progress. In the first therapy session after she received the bad news, Amy said she was shocked at being laid off, and that it seemed overwhelming and even unreal. The topic dominated several subsequent therapy sessions. She felt numb, and had to force herself, or be urged by the therapist, to counteract a tendency towards denial and avoidance. Instead, she gathered together all of the facts about her layoff and what might follow, including making sure that she would obtain unemployment insurance.

Amy did so and set to work applying for a new position. Then she had a phase with intrusive thoughts and fears. She was extremely concerned that even with unemployment insurance her finances would be quickly and totally exhausted. When discussing this fear Amy entered a shimmering state. She spoke rapidly with a rush of one idea after another: her health insurance might stop, she may become ill from stress, her house could be repossessed and she would be thrown out into the street, and people would despise her.

The therapist said after such a cascade, "We have just heard a catastrophic version about what this career change might mean in the future. Perhaps I can guide you, if you would like, in considering where that comes from, and then we can consider three scenarios: this catastrophic version, an ideal version, and then a realistic appraisal of what may lie ahead, in between the two extremes." This technique had worked well earlier in her therapy, so it was not an entirely unfamiliar suggestion about how to make implicit attitudes into explicit conceptualizations.

Amy came to realize that the intrusive images she saw in her mind's eye as she rushed into a cascade of awful consequences to her life from the job loss came from documentaries of the Great Depression. Her parents had suffered through the dust bowl of the plains states and had told her stories when she was growing up of their difficulties and suffeering. That was like a prophecy of doom and made her overestimate the hopelessness of her current career position.

On clarifying the past and present associations with the job loss, and examining further connections, the therapist suggested a plan of slowly going through the ideas that might come to Amy while imagining three scenarios. The first had already been examined: the worst-case scenario for her future identity. Next would be an idealized fantasy scenario, followed by a realistic scenario between catastrophe and fantasy.

The technique of presenting and guiding the patient through several trains of thought operates in several ways. First, it slows down the rush of associated ideas. Second, it clarifies and appraises the ideas in trusted conversations. Third, it links emotions to ideas, and explores how emotions can lead to new coping strategies rather than defensive avoidances.

When the therapist asked for an *ideal imagined future*, Amy had gratifying fantasy images. These overly positive daydreams anticipated that the company that bought the business sector would fire the person who ran their own relevant division and substitute her to do so because she had been so great. She imagined the details of her acceptance of the job offer.

In therapy, these catastrophic and idealized fantasies were then contrasted with *realistic possibilities*. Having the defined plan of looking at three different kinds of scenarios helped Amy manage her emotions enough to process the bad news. As she envisioned the middle ground in between catastrophic and idealized outcomes, she made appraisals of how she could act. This led her towards forming realistic plans and expectations of how to cope with the job change and its impact on her sense of identity.

The three scenarios technique has an additional benefit of promoting attention control. As the patient puts a scenario into words, the patient may have intrusive thoughts. If so, the therapist encourages staying with the scenario rather than following the intrusion. When Amy was trying out the positive fantasy scenario she said intrusive phrases related to the worst-case scenario. The therapist remarked that this was best-case scenario time, which helped Amy stay on track. The therapist can remember the intrusive ideas, and work on them later.

Summary

Once excessive and automatic inhibitions of thinking can be modified, a patient can consciously reflect on habitual attitudes. A patient can develop more hopeful narratives and beliefs, as well as plan more adaptive future behaviors in a similar situation or dilemma. Adaptive thinking leads to a more confident plan of a new course of action. The conscious choice to try something in a new way may require many trials and efforts that at first feel awkward, or even risky. The supportive factor in therapy helps sustain the patient through these uneasy but growth-promoting processes.

9

Defensive styles

Defensive styles are habitual and automatic ways of protecting against pre-viously experienced dangers such as unbearable states of mind and threaten-ing impulses towards action. Most patients have multiple options for self-regulation at their disposal. The choice of which defense to implement may become a trait that worked well enough in the past as a general way of coping with emotional difficulties. A defensive style once useful for coping may have become automatic in adolescence, and may no longer represent an optimal response.

In personality growth, an aim is to develop more conscious controls of emo-tionality. Instead of primitive defenses such as projection operating uncon-sciously, the goal is that a patient learns how to appraise current social situations and make well-reasoned decisions. Instead of global inhibitions, as in constant emotional control, a person ideally learns to express feelings without losing a sense of self-control. Techniques may be used to help the patient to share warm feelings with others.

Observation

Defensive styles are aspects of personality traits. The stylistic pattern of emotional expression and avoidance is repetitive and embedded in relationships, thus the patient may report what significant others observe. For example, a spouse may complain that the patient is too emotionally obtuse, overcontrolled, and remote in sharing feelings.

The clinician is looking for such patterns in recurring stories of various kinds of social interaction and how feelings were felt or avoided (A. Freud, 1936; G. Vaillant, 2009; Horowitz et al., 1992; C. Perry, 2014; Shapiro, 1965; Millon, 1996; McWilliams, 2011; Horowitz, Marmar, Krupnick et al., 2001).

Histrionic patterns are often observed in patients who act out emotions, but have poor conscious awareness of their authentic feelings. *Compulsive* patterns often contain flip-flopping states, in which the patient contradicts himself and is unable to verbalize his emotions. *Narcissistic* patterns are observed in patients who frequently externalize blame to avoid personal shame, and make excessive demands out of a sense of grandiose entitlement. B*orderline* personality disorders may be observed as using a dissociative style of splitting self and other schemas into "all good" and "all bad" configurations. They may suddenly switch from regarding a therapist as an ally to regarding the therapist as an aggressor. The clinician observes a pattern of dissociation between positive and negative feeling states (Gunderson, 2009; Kernberg et al., 2014; Bateman and Fonagy, 2013).

The literature on personality at the level of richness and depth that may be found in intensive single case studies, as in psychoanalysis, has related styles of control in terms of defensive mechanisms. The common ones have become labeled with names such as repression in the common language. These mechanisms are reviewed here, briefly. The order followed below is from those most frequently and easily observed, to others than may be obscure to the observer at first.

Intellectualization

To avoid the problematic emotional implications of a topic, some patients in therapy avoid words for emotions and substitute phases that intellectualize their problems at a theoretical level. A related defense, generalization, involves dealing with a topic on an abstract, rather than a personal level. For example, in a therapy conversation about having cheated while in an honored position of responsibility, a patient may leap to expression of only general philosophical thoughts about human imperfection in order to distance himself from the potential feelings of shame and guilt.

In intellectualization, patients may express emotions regarding a personal experience using a broad social context rather than a personalization ("Ahh, these are the times we live in"). The patient aims to have a social conversation about general ideas rather than giving concrete and specific instances of how he or she is having problems with emotional responses. For instance, a person might report having hit his child, but then sidetrack the conversation by providing views that the therapist might share about the general social values about how punishment and discipline should be provided as part of a child's education

Rationalization

A patient may be observed to maintain self-esteem by rationalization of unhealthy actions such as giving in to intense cravings that ought to have been restrained. Rationalization is also used to avoid unpleasant duties, for example, not completing a chore because of having potentially great, creative thoughts while sitting on the couch watching television.

Reaction formation

By reaction formation, a buried set of ideas or feelings is replaced by an unconsciously derived—but consciously felt—emphasis on its opposite. For example, an older boy who is jealous of a baby brother might harbor a hateful unconscious fantasy that if the baby died, he would again be the center of his parent's attention. He has been told by his parents to love his baby brother. He protects against the dangerous "badness" of self by replacing the wish to be rid of his little brother with an exaggerated kindly concern for the baby's welfare. If the feelings of rivalry are too intense, the reaction formation may lead to problematic symptoms. For instance, the boy might feel a compulsion to check on his baby brother every 15 minutes throughout the night to make sure he is safe from suffocation or rodent attacks. A lifelong trait of over-solicitousness might be developed to ward off envy and jealous hostility.

Disavowal

Denial is one of the most frequent ways of trying to control upsetting ideas and to prevent unbearable emotional states. Denial involves withholding the conscious understanding of meanings and implications of new information. We discussed this as an early general reaction to experiencing a major stressor. Disavowal as a trait means a tendency to use many denials, or protracted denials. For example, upon hearing that company bankruptcy has been declared imminent, a patient might try to achieve peace of mind by assuming, "It can't happen to us," and on hearing that a friend has cancer might say, "Glad it cannot happen in my family."

Idealization

Idealization results from an excessive need to have a relationship, an ideal, or an institution that inflates the patient's sense of worth. This defensive style can counter-act a tendency to enter enfeebled self-states. A fragile self-image is inflated by a sense of union with the ideal. Attributing exaggerated positive qualities to an affiliated person or a group, whether real or imagined, gives that patient a rationalization for their enhanced self-esteem and excitement from the reflected glory.

The results can be serious, as in zealotry and self-sacrifice. Various totalitarian political organizations have profited from this defensive maneuver. When in treatment, such character types are likely to develop positive idealizing transferences that, paradoxically, may interfere with evolving a genuine therapeutic alliance.

Displacement

Displacement occurs when a patient transfers impulses, emotions, or judgments from the actual target person to someone else. It is a "kick the dog" response, for example, when anger is aroused at another family member. For instance, after being reprimanded at work, a person may tactfully submit to the reprimand, yet go home and yell at a child for a minor infraction. The result is a defensive move from the actual target of hostility, who is dangerously stronger than self in power, to choosing a target for aggressive discharge who is weaker than self.

Undoing

Undoing expresses both an impulse and its opposite, such as being domineering one minute and deferential the next. Used in rapid repetition, undoing can lead to a series of flip-flops resulting in a personality trait of indecisiveness. For example, instead of complaining about the frustrating actions of another person, and trying to negotiate an agreement, a patient might start complaining about the other person to the therapist and then too quickly retract the emergent expressions of emotion by saying, "I didn't mean to say that, they meant well."

Repression

Repression differs from suppression, in that *suppression* is a conscious effort aimed to remove attention from a particular theme, memory, or fantasy. Unlike this voluntary process of using attention control consciously, repression results from inhibitions that occur unconsciously. The distinction is useful to make as a part of observations of how a patient handles threatened emergence of emotional topics. Mindfulness training can help a patient learn to use suppression rather than repression, and acceptance rather than supression. This learning becomes a capacity for dose-by-dose thinking about stressful topics: "time on" by engaging attention, alternating with restorative "time off" by disengaging attention and placing attention for a time on a different topic.

A common kind of repressive phenomena can take the form of an inability to consciously remember an important, traumatic event. Alternatively, repression can curb disturbing wishes, ideas, and feelings that have not yet reached consciousness, but would have emerged if not for avoidances. This may include repression of unconscious fantasies. For example, a patient may repress the awareness of revenge impulses directed as a possible future retaliation by a patient upon a parent who was neglectful, harshly punitive, critical, or disapproving (Horowitz, 1997).

Dissociation and splitting

Dissociation involves segregation of concepts that ought to be otherwise more realistically joined into complex forms such as person-schemas. *Splitting* is sometimes defined as the phenomena of "all good" and "all bad" segregations of role-relationship models (Horowitz and Marmar, 1980). Dissociation also refers to a trait of responding to a very threatening moment by lifting away the sense that the self is actually in the situation at hand. The patient deals with painful emotions such as intense fear by temporarily altering the way consciousness works.

The most important observations have to do with dissociation in the sense of splitting apart configurations and holding them in cognitive processing as if unconnected by associations. The consequence is an inaccurate sense of identity. Self and other views can be compartmentalized, as different configurations in a repertoire. What is consciously known in one state of mind is segregated from what is consciously known in another state of mind.

This can be a major cleavage, such as separating views of the self in the world into "all good" or "all bad," or viewing an attachment figure as either "all good" or "all bad," as in constant caretaker versus dangerous predator. A patient who is potentially embarrassed by the selfish act of stealing from a friend can be observed to apparently forget about the time of a minor theft, remembering the relationship only in terms of how the self once promoted a kindly sharing of belongings.

Projection

In the style of projection, a clinician may observe that a patient has taken an intolerable attitude, emotion, or idea and viewed it as if it were active outside of the self, usually in another person. The impulse, feeling, or idea is located as if it were someone else's intention or aim. For example, a patient who struggles to avoid hatred may develop a delusion that others are "out to get them." This gives the patient an acceptable rationale for hostile self-defensive stances even as the projection avoids recognizing internal arousal of the destructive impulses.

In a variation of this, called *projective identification*, a patient may provoke another person into becoming irritable. When the other reacts, one's own anger appears justified as a response to the other person's now hostile behavior. The other is guilty, not the self, of bringing anger into the air. The patient now can feel vindicated in being indignant, and can view the other person as wrong. Therapists may observe the effects as hostile counter-transference feelings in themselves.

Role reversal

In role reversal, the roles of the self and the other are switched. A common reversal is for a patient to place himself in the role of the strong, rather than the weak. For example, when in danger of feeling controlled by the therapist's attempts to focus attention on a useful, but difficult topic, the patient may become domineering and demanding of where attention should be placed.

Another common reversal is to remove self from the role of the accused, and instead become the accuser or critic by blaming the therapist. "You just don't know how to move this therapy along, do you?" is the kind of remark one might observe as a defense against feeling ashamed. When domestic partners both use this defense, they may have volatile, mutually accusatory arguments that extend beyond reasonable limits.

Formulation

Formulation goes beyond the observed repetition of a defensive mode to inferences about how the habit developed. One can infer what functions the defensive style may serve in the present. Formulation also includes the future: how can the patient learn to augment their existing capacities for regulating emotional experiences? These formulations include identification of obstacles to learning in therapy.

Les' projections

Les came into treatment because he eroded or ended his relationships when he encountered even a minor frustration with the other person. He also felt chronic depression that seemed to stem from self-esteem problems. He was a workaholic, but without creative zest. Much of the time, he felt empty and lonely.

When he met someone he felt attracted to because of his or her intelligence, interests, or appearance, Les tended to exhibit a paradoxical response if the other person also showed interest. Instead of feeling excited about the new contact, he felt irritable that what the other person offered did not ideally suit Les' goals.

Even in therapy sessions, he seemed hypersensitive to being engaged in mutually active communication. He seemed to be in a working state when the therapist listened, but when the therapist talked in what might have been a give-and-take kind of conversation, Les was observed to withdraw a bit. If the therapist was flexible and changed his appointment to a more convenient time for Les, his response was paradoxical. Instead of expressing thanks, he appeared sullen and implied that the new time was still inconvenient in relation to his need to work and make money. The therapist began to note in his stories about outside interpersonal contacts that Les felt irritated when the other person seemed to want his company.

Les was able to engage in formulation about this pattern of interpersonal hypersensitivity and paradoxical resentment. When discussing this topic in therapy, Les said that he felt the other was intruding on his time, and even into his mind. He worried that any prospective companion might deplete him. He then backed off, feeling angry with the friend for not providing a better relationship. He tended to project that the other was to blame for relationship degradation, not he.

With this shared formulation, Les realized that his vexation was unrealistic. It was not so unrealistic in the past. He remembered feeling alienated from both his parents during childhood and adolescence. With this developmental formulation he began to feel optimistic about attitude change.

Underneath this pattern in the present and past was what Les came to call "A crazy attitude." This attitude became clear in the immediacy of the therapy frame. To Les, the therapist seemed generous. The therapist gave him what Les could not give to others without feeling empty and depleted by their wishes. He knew intellectually that this was an exaggeration, but it was a familiar one that seemed lifelong to him. The "crazy" part was resenting the therapist for being "better" than himself.

The therapist responded by telling Les that he might challenge his attitude by unpacking all of his ideas related to this resentment. Les tried to cooperate, but introduced every kind of avoidance in a kind of push/pull process. The therapist continued to ask "Why do you feel some resentment towards me?" Gradually, Les explained that this "crazy attitude" was like a security blanket. It protected him from the fear that he would experience warmth in a relationship, only to have it abruptly and painfully jerked away. He resented the therapist for being just about to jerk away the feeling of close connection.

Les wanted the ideal of eternal warmth but had adopted a distant attitude to protect against the reality that no warmth is eternal. The first steps were to learn to tolerate the anxiety of counteracting the "crazy attitude," and become comfortable with the give-and-take process of listening to each other and discussing his feelings. Les had to learn to tolerate some emotional distress at the end of each session, and during anticipation of the therapist's absences for vacations or illnesses.

Knowing that an attitude is irrational is not enough; a familiar irrational attitude must be counteracted by some kind of new learning. This often means tolerating the tension that arises in engaging in new experiences of thought, feeling, and interaction with others.

It helped to have insight, and Les realized he was using attitudes he had developed as a child. Most of the time, Les acted as if he felt normal, performing responsibly and amiably, while simultaneously his inner world felt dark and depressing. He feigned kindness and said the right things, yet he did not feel authentically warm or caring. However, he could not maintain his act when the relationship got closer, when the other person revealed his or her mind to him, and then expected reciprocal disclosure of Les' inner feelings. Part of his darkness, then, was the expectation of the collapse of promising relationships.

Together, Les and the therapist examined the moment of collapse in his relationships through the process of repeatedly and carefully reviewing his memories. He tended to have extreme attitudes, which he called "crazy"—he recognized their extreme, irrational natures. One extreme attitude was that the other person was too intrusive. When he or she tried to be empathic and get closer, Les felt emotionally, almost physically, as if the other person was on the attack invading his mind. If this involved a sexual encounter, this felt to him as if somebody was invading his body.

On the other hand, if the other person moved in a way that Les felt was increasing emotional distance then he interpreted the remoteness as if it were total abandonment. He felt shaky and angry in response to either extreme, closing or distancing in a relationship, leading to his confusing medley of both fear and hostility. Without much room in between the sense of personal space invasion and the relationship rupture, Les had erected defenses to preserve his stronger self-concepts. Others might feel tension or hostility, or be critical. He was an island unto himself, even if a bit socially phobic. In this stance of projecting his negative feelings he could be both alone and intact. This attitude also served as an obstacle to developing more frankness and disclosure in the therapeutic alliance.

To a degree, Les had already learned how to curb his more extreme impulses to act out of hostility, but he had a pattern of shunning the other person as if the other were a kind of aggressor. Now he had to learn to stay in a relationship without expecting to feel mutual warmth, while at the same time, accepting his fear. He had to reduce his defenses against feeling the unpleasantness of relationship uncertainty. By testing the safety of the therapeutic alliance he was learning this kind of new relationship experience.

Through the therapeutic process, he learned to expect and tolerate social fear. At this point, Les could see that he was being neither invaded nor abandoned: if there was some remoteness in the response of the other person, the other person was only having a time-out and would return to tune in to him again. Tolerating threats of fear or embarrassment allowed him to learn new, small techniques to move toward more authentic communion with another person. This allowed him to seek more truthful contact with others. Occasionally, others responded as he hoped, offering closer contact with him. Through this work, Les' behavior of opening up had rewarding outcomes. Sharing these formulations encouraged Les to continue on the path of self-understanding.

Techniques

The therapist's tool bag for modifying defenses and obstacles to therapeutic communication consists of the various ways for establishing safety in the therapeutic alliance. In addition, the therapist focuses attention, often on a moment of avoidance or cognitive distortion. By paying attention, the patient is setting aside an obstacle to self-understanding. That is, the patient learns to use what the therapist says to counteract his automatic internal avoidances and so to reappraise difficult topics.

The major techniques for focusing attention in this way are well known: the therapist repeats what the patient has said, adding nuances that lead to greater clarity and a sense of being understood by the therapist. This fosters the patient's identification with the therapist's way of facing reality, without distortion or excessive trepidation. An emphasis on current safety allows a reduction in the habitual sense of danger that has led to heightened use of defensive styles.

The work in more complex techniques involves counteracting defensive operations. Such techniques call attention to the patient avoiding incipient ideas when the therapist observes avoidant shifts in the patient's dialogue and non-verbal expressions. The goal here is to find signals of defensiveness that, once pointed out, the patient might learn to recognize. The patient is then taught the signals and what they represent. By recognizing what is happening in the present moment the patient may increase insight into why it is happening. New decisions might then be made, opening doors long closed.

A patient may have been talking smoothly, acknowledging with understanding the therapist's contributions to the conversation. Then, anticipated danger looms on the sidelines of the patient's mind, offstage from central conscious decision-making. The patient begins to bluster, speaking louder and faster, moving from specifics to generalities, and looking away from the therapist. The therapist may describe some or all of those observations to the patient, asserting the supposition that this is likely a shift into a defensive state of mind. The patient can feel the shift from smooth talk to blustery talk, and in time, learn to recognize when it happens.

Table 9.1 Observing avoidant behaviors

Locus of signs	Class of signs		
	Discord	Sudden shifts	Sudden shut-offs
Face and body	• Smile on lips with fearful or angry eyes • Tears with smiling mouth	• High rate of change in kind of expression or gesture • Waving away • Head "shake off" • Shoulder "shrug off"	• Scrunched eyes • Pursed lips • Rapid composure from a leakage • Shielding eyes from view
Voice qualities	• Tight sound into monotones • Relaxed tone but with choppy pacing and strange inflections	• High rate of change in kind of expression or gesture • Quavering • Shift to "cancelling out" of prosody	• Sharp inhalation • Halting • Lowering intensity • Narrowing tonalities • Swift softening of inflections
Spoken words	• Incompatible phrases	• Denial after assertion • Obscuring or hedging information	• Filler words • Cut-off parts of words

In this example, the blustering patient speaks both faster and more forcefully in tone. The opposite can also indicate a shift from smooth talk in a working state of mind into a defensive self-state. The patient may shift away from eye contact, stare absently into the therapist's body, slow or cease speaking, speak softly, repeat syllables, or form a non-expressive, mask-like countenance. Often, these acts signal efforts to avoid what otherwise might be expressed. Some of these signs are summarized in Table 9.1.

It may help to tell patients why signs of defensiveness have been called to their attention. One goal, which the therapist can explain, is slowing down the appraisal of what is happening in the here and now. Slowing down means the expansion of conceptual space, allowing many concepts to come forth.

Metaphorically, slowing down allows the patient to open up a non-critical theater in the mind, a stage on which multiple actors may speak. This also involves letting the usually offstage critics speak their parts of the dialogue, with the therapist maintaining a non-judgmental, equidistant attitude from all of the "speakers."

The therapist aims to increase safety by helping the patient express emotional concepts without becoming disorganized. Learning to pay attention in a productive way includes practicing the skills for engaging in expression and discussion of potentially distressing topics and, if there is too much emotional arousal, disengaging and moving for a time to another topic. In therapy, the clinician senses how much expression the patient is likely to tolerate, and he or she assists the control of joint attention. This is a dose-by-dose kind of exposure and can, to an extent, soothe expectations of having too much emotion on a theme. It is an aspect of desensitization of a traumatic memory by reviewing it in multiple contexts.

For example, the patient may simply stop the progression of ideas. Instead of clarifying certain themes, a patient may say "I don't know"—in other words, "I don't want to know." The therapist functions to counteract that impulse, behaving in a way that expresses the idea, "Let us see if we can now tolerate the exploration and understanding of that topic together, allowing some unpleasant feelings, but feeling safe to do so."

Summary

Eventually, over the course of therapy, the patient learns better ways of controlling their states of mind. The result is more spontaneity and expanded explorations of meaning. In this process, the patient is encouraged by an intuitive sense of increasing solidity and better grounding of a sense of identity. They ideally feel more attached to others because of increased empathy and compassion for them.

10

Emotional avoidance maneuvers

Ideally the therapist fosters safe, metered expression of emotional topics. When the therapist believes the patient needs to stop avoidance maneuvers, additional techniques to focus attention are used. By learning to control emotion without avoiding communication of feelings, the patient can explore topics that have been difficult to process. The patient learns to bring reactions to stress, trauma, and loss to a point of completion and ultimately mastery. Equally important, many patients have limited closeness and constancy in relationships because they present a personality trait of overly controlled emotional expression to others. In therapy, fostered by the therapist's interventions to counteract excessive avoidance, they learn to safely express a richer tapestry of feelings.

In this chapter, the focus will be on observing excessive avoidance, formulating what might be going on in the patient's conscious and unconscious mental processes, and safely challenging the patient's excessive defenses.

The therapist may observe signs of avoidance without understanding the unwanted subject. The goal of counteracting avoidance is twofold: to discover and advance work on these underlying meanings, as well as to help the patient learn new ways of maintaining well-modulated states of mind.

Observation

The therapist observes both the verbal and non-verbal flow of messages from the patient, as well as the therapist's own reactions. The following is an example of a therapist observing avoidance and reacting to it. The patient and therapist were focusing attention on the memory of a recent upsetting argument between the patient and his adolescent son. The patient felt angry then, but right now in therapy the patient was being unclear about who was angry and why. Probably both father and son were angry but instead of labeling the emotions the patient told the therapist peripheral details in an intellectualizing manner that was part of his long-standing defensive style.

The therapist told the patient that he observed him start out by clearly describing his feelings about the episode, but right in the present moment he seemed to avoid elaborating on his feelings. The patient continued with details, but began slowing down, having many pauses, taking back some ideas he just put forward, and going around and about while juggling ideas of who, he or his son, might have been to blame. Then the patient said he was sorry he became angry at his son and seemed to want to get off the topic altogether, as if that concluded discussion. The therapist said, "I am not sure if I am following you on what happened. Am

I correct in thinking your son had done something wrong, you were admonishing him, and he disagreed with you, upon which you felt angry at him?"

The patient replied forcefully, "No, of course I was not too irritated with him!" This remark was an avoidance of (1) emotions regarding the argument with his son, and (2) how he felt currently talking about it with the therapist. What the therapist felt intuitively, observing his own reactions, was that the patient was feeling shame in the present moment for expressing too much anger in the memory of the argument with his son. And the patient was incipiently angry with the therapist for exposing him to potential embarrassment if he told the story completely. The therapist knew that avoidance was taking place, and could formulate some, but not all, of the underlying reasons.

The therapist chose to challenge the patient with a somewhat paradoxical reflection of what the patient had last said. The therapist said, "Oh, so of course you were not very irritated with him, I guess maybe he was the one who was angrier at you?" The patient stayed on the topic and added more information. Patient and therapist clarified together that both father and son were angry.

That work led the patient to say he regretted how he had spoken angrily. He experienced and then told the therapist about emotions related to his embarrassment in the present moment with the therapist. He felt he had lapsed in control of his anger in the argument with his son, and been overly harsh in his criticism.

This conversational passage stayed within the frame of a therapeutic alliance, without transference feelings of any intensity, and the patient and the therapist were moving forward in understanding the memory and what it now meant. The therapist was now observing, after a too-avoidant passage, an adaptive level of control over the emergent sense of shame.

This example illustrates a therapist observing avoidant maneuvers and their consequences. Although the patient did not exhibit failure of emotional regulation, he did exhibit avoidance as well as shame around the argument with his son. During the conversation with the therapist, the patient advanced to an adaptive use of his capacities to control the topic being communicated.

A general review of such avoidant maneuvers aimed at emotional control that might be observed in following a patient's present-moment communication in words is depicted in Table 10.1. The table has categories of observable outcomes. In this and in all tables that follow, categories of process are listed vertically and observable outcomes are indicated horizontally. These outcomes are also loosely categorized as excessive avoidance, adaptive control, and failing to stifle unwanted feelings (failures of regulation).

The first type of maneuver in the table is topic selection. In the previous example, the patient exhibited an avoidant moment when he attempted to change the *topic of attention* in therapy away from the memory. The second type of maneuver involves altering the expressed concepts of a specific topic. This maneuver was observed when the patient stayed on the topic of attention, but altered the concepts about his anger: he said he was angry, and then attempted to take it back. The outcome of this alteration of concepts seemed to the therapist to be overly avoidant.

Table 10.1 Content of communication: Outcomes of avoidance maneuvers

Maneuver	Outcomes		
	Adaptive control	Too-avoidant	Failure of regulation
Altering Topics of Attention	Expresses a potentially stressful topic to a degree that both self and therapist can tolerate the evoked emotion.	Does not present stressful topic(s) and instead selects obscuring or misleading alternative topic(s).	Suddenly plunges too far into expressing emotionally overwhelming topic.
Altering Concepts	Communicates key facts and emotions; contemplates implications and possible solutions to problems; alert to remarks of therapist.	Conceptual reluctance; misleads others who are potentially helpful; gives misinformation; provides generalized discussion when specifics are indicated. Avoids expressing a concept that might prove useful in solving problems; switches facts back and forth; ignores remarks of therapist.	Fragments of sensations and ideas are disjointedly presented.
Altering the Importance to Self in a Chain of Concepts	As the patient speaks, the importance of the topic to self becomes clearer.	Saves face at the expense of rational recognitions.	Disruptive or chaotic shifts in appraisals.
Altering Threshold for Disengagement	Opens and closes a topic as helps contemplation.	Alters attention to terminate a tense state prematurely.	Unable to control the focus of attention or follow therapist's efforts to do so.

Although at first the patient was disavowing anger, he soon moved into what seemed to the therapist as an *adaptive level of control of emotion*. The patient also reported that during the argument with his son he had experienced a relative *failure of emotional regulation*, expressing too much anger.

Maneuvers to control emotion may also affect the tone and manner in which a patient expresses ideas and emotions. Perhaps the most frequent observation of this kind concerns discord between verbal and non-verbal messages. In the above example, the patient may have said that he was not angry with his son, not now and not then, and not angry with the therapist in the present moment, but his non-verbal messages were discordant because he was glaring at the therapist,

Table 10.2 Forms of communication: Outcomes of avoidance maneuvers

Maneuver	Outcomes		
	Adaptive control	Too-avoidant	Failure of regulation
Altering Mode of Representation	Coherent mix of talk, facial expression, imagery metaphor, and gesture.	Disruptive image metaphors; flat verbiage; discordant messages across words, voice, face, and body.	Too intense expression of somatic emotion without talk about the meaning or context.
Altering Time Frame	Coherent framing of time as to past, present, future, or imaginary perspectives.	Disruptive or confusing shifts in temporal perspective.	Chaotic time jumps.
Altering Focus on Reality vs. Fantasy	Balance between rational planning and fantasy; restorative humor.	Disruptive or confusing shifts between analytic reasoning and fantasy; avoidant humor.	Inability to follow a thread of reasoning.
Altering Level of Action Planning	Appropriate choices of when to speak and when to listen.	Avoidant disruption of turn-taking in a dialog; restless bodily jittering to avoid thinking and feeling.	Impulsively excessive actions or "word salad."
Altering Arousal Level	Appropriate moments of lulls and activations.	Excessive speed or slowing to avoid useful attention focusing.	Excessive agitation.

clenching and unclenching his fist, and raising his voice. The therapist might wonder if there was a danger of the patient becoming flooded with rage, but was observing avoidance behaviors that might function to prevent that from happening.

Later in the resumption of a working state, the patient displayed adaptive control: he expressed anger, remorse, shame, and acceptance emotions in harmony between verbal and non-verbal messages.

Table 10.1 concerned observations of verbal contents of what the patient says. The form of the communication is also important as an aspect of kinds of emotional regulation. Several such ways of regulating forms of communication are described in relation to observable consequences in Table 10.2.

Another category concerns how controlling maneuvers may alter the relative activation of self and other schemas. For example, a patient avoiding the mourning process for his brother who had committed suicide a decade earlier, seemed about to express guilt that he had been callous in dealing with the brother's urgent requests for his attention. At that moment of incipient emotion, he switched his attitude and told the therapist he had been too weak to help his brother's distress. This maneuver avoided the incipient feelings of guilt by switching to potential feelings of shame at his weakness. But before shame could be expressed, he switched away from the "I was just too weak" concept. His authentic emotions remained suppressed as a consequence of these flip-flops in apparent self-appraisals.

Several communicative maneuvers to control views of self and other, and their observable consequences in therapy communications, are summarized in Table 10.3. The case just discussed also exemplifies an avoidant alteration of role-relationship models, and that will be discussed further, below, under the formulation heading.

Formulation

A patient may express their thoughts enough for the therapist to infer how the patient may be controlling emotional arousal in the patient's own mind. Sometimes these intra-psychic inferences are useful to share observations and formulations with the patient. Using reflective self-awareness, the patient can alter attention, intending to engage what may come up next, and thus modify an unconscious avoidance maneuver.

That is, some patients who have good reflective self-awareness can benefit from the therapist clarifying maneuvers that are not entirely conscious, but that could be counteracted by conscious intentions to do so.

For example, in Table 10.1 on the control of topics of attention, the outcome of avoidance (*does not present stressful topics and instead selects obscuring or misleading alternative topics*) could be shared with the patient. In the last example, the therapist could say to the patient avoiding the topic of his brother's suicide, "It seems to me that you start to touch upon, but really stay away from presenting information on your brother's suicide."

The therapist could also share with the patient their guess of what may be taking place in the patient's mind. In some patients, that may work better. Sharing guesses or inferences of the patient's mental operations can help them to counteract avoidance by bringing attention to the subject, as well as to enhance their capacity for self-reflective awareness in general. The therapist could say:

"I am guessing that you avoid thinking about your brother's suicide, which functions as a kind of denial of a topic that requires attention but that you have avoided because you do not want to experience the associated painful emotions."

Table 10.1 summarized some categories of observing control of the contents of verbal communications during therapy dialogues. The same categories can be used to formulate the processes that may be going on in the patient's mind. That inference about often preconscious mental processes leading to conscious mental

Table 10.3 Person-schemas that organize communication: Outcomes of avoidance maneuvers

Maneuvers Outcomes	Outcomes		
	Adaptive control	Too-avoidant	Failure of regulation
Altering Self-Schemas	Coherent self-presentation.	Jarring shifts in apparent personality.	Chaotic fragments and depersonalization states.
Altering Schema of Other Person	Increases understanding of the intentions, motives, and predictable patterns of other (empathy); ability to "read" another during an interaction; holds a stable view of who the other is.	Provokes the other to conform to an internal misperception; short circuits to an inappropriate all-good or all-bad view of other; changes the object of a feeling, wish, or source of threat from the most pertinent one to a less pertinent one.	Chaotic or extreme irrational views about what to expect from others.
Altering Role-Relationship Models	Useful trials of a new scenario for a situation.	Preservation of a rigid view of the situation, rather than acting flexibly as the situation unfolds; switches working models between dichotomies such as all-good or all-bad views of the relationship; changes the source of an activity, wish, or feeling from self to other, or other to self.	Inability to use alliance to stabilize discourse.
Altering Values	Follows values, rules, and commitments.	Irrationally attributes blame outwardly to protect self-esteem.	Enraged reactions, as if therapist is rule-breaking.
Altering Executive Agency Schema	Acts responsibly to care for others and to care for self as a situation demands.	Extremes of selfish or self-sacrificing acts.	Inability to responsibly care for self.

Table 10.4 Contents of conscious experience: Outcomes of avoidance maneuvers

Maneuvers	Defensive outcomes		
	Adaptive control	Too-avoidant	Failure of regulation
Altering Topics of Attention	Useful periods of contemplating and not contemplating emotional topic.	Topics of importance are not examined; needed decisions are not made; forgetting, disavowal, or denial of a topic that requires attention.	Intrusion of an emotionally overwhelming topic.
Altering Concepts	Useful contemplation of implications and possible solutions to problems; selective inattention to vexing or distressing concepts in order to gain restoration from distressing levels of emotion.	Avoids key concepts; moves from the emotional heart of a topic to its periphery; leaves cause-and-effect sequences distorted or obscured.	Disjointed thought: failure to test reality of appraisals.
Altering the Importance to Self in a Chain of Concepts	Weighs alternatives and accepts the best solution to a problem amongst alternatives; accepts realistic estimates; appropriate humor.	Irrational exaggeration or minimization; rationalizes alternative solutions that are less rational than other solutions.	Chaotic shifts in attitude: lack of clarity about who has which beliefs.
Altering Threshold for Disengagement	Takes action when a good solution has been reached; tolerates high levels of negative emotion without derailing a topic.	Terminates contemplation of a topic prematurely.	Too quickly reaches irrational conclusions.

experiences is summarized in Table 10.4, a companion to Table 10.1 in terms of the processes involved.

In the same manner, the "intra-psychic" companion to Table 10.2, which was on the form of communication, is Table 10.5, which shows the intra-psychic *forms* of thinking that organize internal experiences and thus regulate the emergence of potential emotions. Presenting conscious representations only in words has different emotional consequences than presenting them in both words and sensory images.

In addition to the form and content of thoughts, control processes can change the activation of *person schemas* in a repertoire. These intra-psychic operations

Table 10.5 Forms of conscious experience: Outcomes of avoidance maneuvers

Maneuvers	Outcomes		
	Adaptive control	Too-avoidant	Failure of regulation
Altering Mode of Representation	Selective representation in verbal, imagery, and somatic modes.	Omission of useful modes; excessive numbing by avoiding images; avoids understanding images in words; prolonged escapist use of daydreaming.	Intrusive and excessively vivid images; disruptively intense bodily sensations from raw emotions.
Altering Time Frame	Ability to focus on an appropriate time frame. Looks at plans one step at a time to avoid being emotionally overwhelmed by long-term implications.	Denies urgency of a threat; disavows long-range implications to self; focuses on past or future to avoid the need to make present decisions and take necessary actions.	Chaotic sense of sequences of memories.
Altering Focus on Reality vs. Fantasy	Balance between rational planning and restorative or creative fantasy.	Excessive preoccupation with fantasy or with small, logical steps and details.	Confusion.
Altering Level of Action Planning	Restorative changes between logical analysis and fantasy, and between activity and thought; readiness to plan for prompt action at appropriate signs of opportunity; useful restraint.	Preoccupation with escapist daydreams; thinking to avoid important perceptions; preoccupation with perception to avoid necessary thinking; excessive action to avoid thought; excessive thought to avoid decision-making; paralysis of action in favor of endless rumination.	Impulsive action and/or thought; too few conceptual lines of rational thinking.
Altering Arousal Level	Balance between arousal and rest cycles.	Excessive vigilance and compulsive worry; excessive time in sleeping, reverie, and lethargy.	Frenzied or exhausted states of mind.

Table 10.6 Schemas that organize conscious experience: Outcomes of avoidance Maneuvers

Maneuvers	Outcomes		
	Adaptive control	Too-avoidant	Failure of regulation
Altering Self-Schemas	Examining various self-appraisals and harmonizing them to form a coherent sense of identity.	Excessively grand beliefs about self to ward off negative self-views; excessively negative views of self to justify giving up; shifting "sub-personalities."	States of chaotic fragmentation of self-organization
Altering Schema of Other Person	Enriched understanding of the intentions, motives, and predictable patterns of other.	Attributions of other that seem distorted in order to divest self of blame.	Impoverished understanding of the intentions of the therapist.
Altering Role-Relationship Models	Resilient change in internal working model of a current situation.	Reverses roles inappropriately: All-good or all-bad views. Irrationally changes the agent or source of feeling from self to other.	Annihilation anxiety or panic on separations.
Altering Value Schemas	Sagacious monitoring of the rules that apply to situations.	Unrealistic devaluation or idealization of self and/or other; switches values with the appetites of the moment.	Inability to evaluate moral consequences.
Altering Executive-Agency Schema	Restorative sense of being a part of something beyond self.	Excessive surrender of best interests of self; excessive self-centeredness.	States of irresponsibility and helplessness.

and consequences are shown in Table 10.6, which complements the more communication-oriented observations of Table 10.3 with mental operations.

The important thing about Tables 10.1–10.6 is the general principle of observing what is going on in communication (Tables 10.1–10.3) and formulating what may be going on in the patient's mind. Of course, to some extent the patient may report conscious experiences, but in actual experience they do not always do so, and in addition many of the processes are preconscious rather than conscious. Some salient references for the outcomes described include Perry, Augusto, & Cooper, 1989; Singer, 1990; Vaillant, 1994; Conte & Plutchik, 1995; Saklofske & Zeidner, 1995; Horowitz, Znoj, & Stinson, 1996; Horowitz, Reidbord et al., 1994; Reidbord et al., 1993; Horowitz, Cooper et al., 1992; Horowitz & Stinson, 1995; Horowitz, Znoj, & Stinson, 1996; Horowitz, 1988a, 1988b, 1998, 2011, 2014; Horowitz, Markman et al., 1990.

Technique

The observations and formulations that detect moments, in therapy, of excessive avoidance are useful because learning to make these observations and inferences leads to an advanced intuition of when it is safe to intervene. Techniques that counteract avoidance lead to processing the avoided emotions and underlying meanings.

Such interventions include calling the moment of avoidance to the patient's attention, as well as asking the patient about the thwarted topic. A therapist might say, "You were talking about [name the concepts] and I wonder if there is more to that." Multiple interventions are used to clarify what the avoidance was and why it seemed necessary then and may not be required now, because the patient can tolerate the potential emotions.

The following is a case example to illustrate such present moment in psychotherapy techniques. By unfreezing a warded-off topic related to grief over the death of his brother, mourning was able to advance, and in addition capacities of Ben were enhanced. In other words, Ben was able to arrive at more adaptive narration of his past and modify personality traits of emotional over-control.

Ben

Ben was in his mid-thirties when he came to treatment. He complained of feeling stagnant, unsatisfied, and anxious about his future career and family life. He worked in middle management and experienced difficulty in feeling good about following or giving directions in relation to co-workers. It was time for a promotion, but he wondered about how he was being assessed. His self-esteem fluctuated widely. He was socially active, but in a highly intellectual style of engagement that others perceived as emotionally over-controlled.

Ben was motivated to change through the feeling of support from the relationship with the clinician during therapy. His goals were clarified. He wanted to improve his functioning at work and in relationships. He knew that he sometimes made trouble for himself by trying to control others excessively, or being remote to prevent them from having power over his life. He reported similar concerns, including power and status struggles, in and between his parents and siblings. He felt ambivalent about most members of his family but could not express this clearly early in treatment.

He was single and wanted to marry and have a family. No relationship moved well in that direction. Too often he was over-controlling and seemed remote so the woman broke off the relationship. Yet he felt an inability to tolerate interdependence. This pattern meant that he did well enough in preliminary encounters, but then remained too distant when challenged to meet some requests from a partner. He knew philosophically he had to be able to both lead and follow in what might become a domestic partnership. His lack of capacity to do so motivated him for the hard work of analyzing relationship transactions, and memories, during therapy.

He worked well in therapy, examining the story of some ruptured relationships with women he had liked. A cycle of states was clarified. First he would enter a state of interest in common activities that might be shared with another person. Then as closeness increased he felt tense and then remote, possibly disrupting the relationship. With separation he felt less anxious, but then more depressed and lonely. He would then seek companionship again.

A somewhat similar pattern was identified at work. Ben manifested uncertainty about his sense of identity. He oscillated between roles as stronger or weaker in position of power in relation to others. He felt stronger than others in his keen intelligence. He felt inferior because he had not reached a career pinnacle and because a birth defect had left him with a limp.

Sometimes he felt he was inferior to the therapist. Sometimes he felt he was in charge and the therapist followed after. Sometimes he felt ambivalent about the therapist, such as exhibiting momentary annoyance or "wanting more than what was given." These transference feelings were not intense and did not interfere with working states.

In a session of mid-therapy he reported that a family reunion had triggered thoughts of his older brother who he had scarcely mentioned to the therapist up to this point in time. This brother had committed suicide a decade earlier. The reunion was followed by days of intrusive thoughts connecting present issues with past family transactions, especially around the time and consequences of his brother's suicide. The therapist formulated the possibility of a frozen, complex grief reaction.

In a subsequent session the therapist tried to focus attention on the story of the relationship with his brother, and the meaning of the loss to Ben. Ben focused instead on a problem with his current dating life. Observing the avoidance maneuver, and having an initial tentative formulation, the therapist said, "It seems to me, right now, that you are interrupting potential trains of thought about your brother's death that might be important for us to understand. What do you think?"

In response, Ben said firmly, "I don't think that is relevant to me now. It was a long time ago. I stopped thinking about him." Ben had dismissed the therapist's suggestion with non-verbal messages that suggested that he was feeling in a strong self-state in regard to the therapist's weaker concepts of what might be important. Ben then changed his self-state. He assumed a less dominating posture, and curled forward. He stopped being dogmatic. With some signs of halting speech, Ben then revealed to the therapist more about how he had been reluctant to disclose to close friends that his brother had even died. In fact some acquaintances of his still believed that his brother was still alive. He was afraid of their asking how the brother died. He did not want to say by suicide.

This remark helped clarify the therapist's formulation of what might be avoided. Ben had potential feelings of embarrassment in revealing the suicide to long-standing acquaintances, causing the therapist to stay on the topic. The therapist said, "Yes, I certainly can understand your predicament, you do need to correct your story with people who know you because it can feel more and more embarrassing to account for your delay in telling them that your brother is dead, even more so how he died. I think you might feel there is stigma from his suicide."

Ben winced at the word suicide, fell silent, and looked away, then back. He began concealing his face with his hand. Finally he began looking quizzically at the therapist, who chose to break the silence by saying, "And right now perhaps we should consider that embarrassment may threaten you. You winced when I said 'he had committed suicide.' Let us just suppose that might be embarrassing for you."

Ben did not respond. He straightened up, manifesting a firm, strong bodily posture in the chair. Then he spoke again. He seemed to enter an over-modulated state within which he depreciated the therapist's efforts to help him focus attention on the brother because it happened too long ago.

The therapist said, "Ten years is a long time and you have been moving along, developing yourself. And I think we have been doing good work in therapy. But I must tell you that you seem to be avoiding a review right now of what happened. Maybe I am wrong and now is not a good time to go into this, but I think something of your relationship with your brother lives on in your mind. Maybe you are trying to keep away from some emotional ideas."

Ben said firmly and a bit scornfully, "You don't think I'm done with all that?!"
The therapist calmly and softly replied, "I think maybe not, maybe not."
Ben said, "Humph!"

After a momentary silence, Ben went on to talk about a current work crisis. Ben was in effect saying that the therapist was on the wrong track in asking questions related to the suicide (therefore intellectually weaker than him). Then a flip occurred, and a change back into a shimmering state of mind. He went back to what the therapist had suggested: "What I do find embarrassing is that I feel like I am kind of putting you down. After all, you are a respected therapist and I certainly do not have such expertise."

He continued in various commentaries about psychotherapy as a career, using intellectualization. He shifted states rapidly. For a time he strongly deprecated the therapist's suggestions of where to pay attention. Then he shifted to a weakly obsequious stance, while insincerely seeming to explore themes suggested for attention by the therapist. Neither of the alternating role-relationship models were cooperative. He was either strong and the therapist relatively weak, or he was bowing to the therapist's directions and himself in a stance that was relatively weak.

Eventually he resumed talking about his brother more frankly. Now he was switching between three role relationship models; self as weaker than the controlling therapist, self as strong and talking about whatever he wanted, and a therapeutic alliance role relationship model of jointly cooperating in exploring his current issues. The session ended, and he shook his head with some dissatisfaction as he strode firmly out of the office.

Ben started the next therapy session by telling the therapist that he did not understand why he just started having intrusive images related to memories of himself at age five after the last session. This was like a waking dream, not a night dream. He wondered why these unbidden images popped up at this particular time. The therapist asked for detailed descriptions and associations.

Ben did allow himself fuller expression, but often retracted some comment he had just made by saying, "No, that was of no importance."

The therapist said, "You want to wipe the screen clear rather than having some kind of impending, emerging feeling." Ben seemed to feel invigorated, then, for more exploration. He went on with further description of the images that had come unbidden into his mind since the previous session.

In one intrusive image, Ben saw himself as five years old, bumping clumsily into a stranger on the street and being shamed by his father's angry, accusatory voice because his father felt socially embarrassed by having others see that he had a handicapped son. He experienced this as an irritating form of selfishness on his father's part. He felt his father despised him because father was a great athlete, and his brother, with a perfect body, had athletic promise.

The relationship with his father had been a topic in clarifying his maladaptive patterns, his ambivalence, his emotional over-control, and his self-criticism. Now he repeated an aspect of the previous formulations. He added that he felt his father had been remote from him and had been less remote to his brother. Ben had felt closer to his brother than anyone else in the family. At the time Ben was becoming more successful, his brother was failing. Ben did not want to be dragged down into a state of discouragement. He felt the brother should take charge of his own life, and let Ben lead his life quite independently. While talking about having become distant from his brother Ben seemed at that moment to realize that he did not want to talk about the suicide but maybe he should do so anyway. The therapist asked Ben to tell him more about his brother's death.

The brother had called him for help just a day before he was found dead. Ben had important work to do that day and declined to make time to see him. In retrospect, his brother had needed more support. In his intrusive image Ben as a five year old needed close support from his father. Ben had not contemplated the association between the intrusive images of this childhood memory and the suicide, but now did so. Father was to blame for being critical, Ben was to blame for insisting too strongly that brother and he should each be "perfectly independent."

Feeling hesitant but safe, Ben said his decision to work despite his brother's plea for help was bad, that he was being too strong in pursuing his career, which had harmed his brother. This approximation of the idea of working, and the enduring attitude that selfishness was bad because it harmed others, led him to feel guilty.

Experiencing this emotion during therapy dialogue, he was observed to have a facial expression of self-disgust and he then uttered a low moan.

To avoid the danger of being flooded with remorse, he had inhibited this sequence of concepts from expression. Now he expressed, in words, his feelings of remorse for not going to see his brother right away. Ben stayed in shimmering and well-modulated states in the therapy session.

Ben and the therapist jointly formulated that the intrusive images of his distress on the street with his father at age five was a way for the avoided and unresolved memory of his brother's suicide to gain conscious representation. He could now continue grief work and begin a new narrative. He expressed more fully ideas of anger at his brother for bringing shame to the family. Their community believed suicide was immoral. That is why he had not told his own acquaintances about his brother.

In therapy he had the insight that being angry now with his brother for committing suicide served the purpose of keeping him from feeling shame and guilt. The reaction of shame stemmed from ideas of the "weakness" of imperfection and failure held by his family and community. Hi guilt, of course, stemmed from responding to his brother's request to see him just the day before the death. Instead he had "strongly" focused on his own work because he wanted to go forward and achieve success. How could he feel good about this ambition? It seemed selfish, as he viewed his father too as selfish.

He then expressed views of himself as stronger than his brother in intellectual capacities and accomplishments although his brother was stronger in body. Moreover, Ben believed that his brother committed suicide because of despair about failures resulting from inadequate intelligence. Ben was able to construct a story of himself as competing with his brother for achievement and praise.

In the specific topic of the relationship with his brother, it now appeared that Ben's states of mind had followed a series of shifts and a sequence of interaction. (1) The weaker man (brother) asked the stronger competent man (self) for help. (2) The self ignored the plea for self-centered reasons, and (3) the brother signaled that he had been harmed by neglect. (4) The self expressed no remorse. Then (5) the reappraising self judged the previously acting self as bad for being strong and, like his father, too selfish. This led to (6) a defensive role reversal, with a shred of reality, as he was weak (in body) and the brother should have been the strong one, being physically sound and receiving more positive attention from their father. The brother should have tolerated the predicaments of life. So the brother could be blamed for the suicide and Ben could be angry at him.

Because it contained a complex medley of shame, rage, fear, guilt, and sadness, this narrative had been hard to understand as a linear story because Ben had not wanted to experience the emotions that would accompany a full conscious review. Re-narration in conversation gradually overcame his avoidance maneuvers. *Doing so allowed Ben to learn how to tolerate negative feeling states. He revised attitudes involving remorse, guilt, love, anger, and shame.*

Let us review several avoidance operations that were observed and then counteracted by the therapist. Ben shifted away from the topic of his brother. Within the topic of his brother he moved away from the concepts about the suicide that excited emotion. Ben used forms of communication and thinking that emphasized intellectual meanings. He used few words for feeling states. Ben also habitually shifted schemas to undue emergent feelings. As a defense against feeling too strong, selfish, and guilty, he reversed roles. He activated another schema in which he was the vulnerable, handicapped one as in the intrusive image being disparaged by his father. He was a weak child, blaming his father for self-preoccupation rather than caring for his sons. The therapist brought attention to these avoidance maneuvers and then clarified the averted feelings.

Interpretations and clarifications followed these conflicting self-concepts: Ben had wish-fear-defense configurations in both his too-strong and too-weak self-schematizations. He oscillated between them whenever he had to soothe unpleasant emotions. Unpleasant emotions can work defensively, as in anger counteracting guilt and *vice versa*. Rather than self-reflective awareness, Ben would feel upset, confused, and change the topic in his mind and in therapy conversations. The two somewhat dissociated polarities were as follows.

In a strong position of self, he wished to become a skillful, great man who refused to be hindered by his own handicap or to help his brother instead of accomplishing some promising task. He feared accusations of having abandoned his brother, calling out vainly for him. He defended his self-esteem by inhibiting his thought processes about the loss of his brother, and avoiding closeness with others, focusing on his work and being self-promoting (like his father). As an outcome of this defensive stance he did not tell acquaintances of his brother's death and responded to them as if he were still alive.

In a weak position of self, he wished to be close with his brother when the brother was a strong athlete and before the brother's career failures. As the weaker brother, less admired by the athletic father, Ben feared that staying close to his brother left him in the shadow. Instead of using his superior intelligence he would remain trapped in a lower status in the future. This caused anxiety about his identity stability. His defense in this polarity was to switch back to the strong polarity just summarized. But when he had thoughts of being stronger than his brother, he felt pangs of shame and guilt. To protect from this danger, his defense was to switch back to the weak polarity of self.

The therapist helped him counteract flip-flopping between these extremes of self as much weaker or much stronger than another person. This allowed a reappraisal of ideas about how to join and harmonize role-relationship models other than repeatedly switching his interpretations of what was going on between the extremes at his strong and weak polarities. Ben, operating within a therapeutic alliance, learned to think of cooperative strength, and non-degrading weakness. As he reduced his habitual tendency to dichotomous thinking, he developed a more harmonious middle ground of who he was and what he wanted in relationships with others.

Ben was able to rethink the story of himself and his brother. Complementary progress occurred on other topics. He developed more enduring intimate relationships with women, had warm rather than cold reunions with his mother and father, and had states of cooperation even in the necessarily competitive relationships he had with work peers, superiors, and subordinates. As such personality growth occurred, his self-esteem improved. He experienced less anxiety and remorse, and fewer depressive moods.

Summary

This chapter reviewed a variety of consequences and observable control operations. When too much avoidance of potential emotions is observed, the therapist can consider if timing is right to intervene by countering the avoidance maneuvers. Then the patient may continue on a topic that otherwise might be derailed. Within this enriched self-reflective experience, patients can gain better self-esteem, closer relationships, and more functional ways of coping consciously with their own emotional potentials.

References

Ainsworth, M.D.S. (1979). Infant-mother attachment. *American Psychologist*. 34, 932–937.

American Psychiatric Association. (2013). *Diagnostic and statistical manual of mental disorders* (5th ed.). Arlington, VA: American Psychiatric Publishing.

Aron, L. (1996). *A meeting of minds: Mutuality in psychoanalysis*. Hillsdale, NJ: Analytic Press.

Atwood, G. E. & Stolorow, R. D. (1984, 2014). *Structures of subjectivity: Explorations in psychoanalytic phenomenology and contextualism*. London & New York: Routledge.

Averill, J. R. (1983). Studies on anger and aggression: Implications for theories of emotion. *American Psychologist, 38*, 1145–1160.

Bateman, A. & Fonagy, P. (2013). Mentalization-based treatment. *Psychoanalytic Inquiry, 33*(6), 595–613. doi:10.1080/07351690.2013.835170.

Bateman, A.W. and Fonagy, P. (2004). Mentalization-based treatment of BPD. *Journal of Personality Disorders, 18*(1), 36–51.

Bateman, A.W. and Fonagy, P. (2004). Mentalization-based treatment of BPD. *Journal of Personality Disorders, 18*(1), 36–51.

Beck, A. (1976). Cognitive therapy and the emotional disorders. New York: International Universities Press.

Bender, D.S., Morey, L.C., Skodol, A.E. Toward a model for assessing level of personality functioning in DSM-5, part I: A review of theory and methods. *J Pers Assess*. 2011 Jul; 93(4):332–46.

Benjamin, L. S. (1979). Structural analysis of differentiation failure. *Psychiatry: Journal For The Study Of Interpersonal Processes, 42*(1), 1–23.

Benjamin, L. S. (1987). Use of the SASB dimensional model to develop treatment plans for personality disorders: I. Narcissism. *Journal of Personality Disorders, 1*(1), 43–70.

Benjamin, L. S. (1996). A clinician-friendly version of the Interpersonal Circumplex: Structural Analysis of Social Behavior (SASB). *Journal of Personality Assessment, 66*(2), 248–266.

Benjamin, L. S. (2003). *Interpersonal reconstructive therapy: Promoting change in non-responders*. New York, NY, US: Guilford Press.

Berridge, K. & Winkielman, P. (2003). What is an unconscious emotion? *Cognition & Emotion, 17*, 181–211.

Beuchler, S. (2008). *Making a difference in patients' lives: Emotional experience in the therapeutic setting*. New York: Routledge, Taylor & Francis Group.

Bion, W. R. (1962). The psychoanalytic study of thinking. *International Journal of Psycho-Analysis, 43*, 306–310.

Bion, W.R. (1967). Notes on memory and desire. *Psychoanalytic Forum*, 2, 279–281.

Bion, W.R. (1997). *Taming wild thoughts*. London: Karnac Books.

Bohleber, W., Fonagy, P., Jimenez, J.P., Scarfone, D., Varin, S., Zysman, S. (2013). Towards a better use of psychoanalytic concepts: A model illustrated using the concept of enactment. *Int. J. Psycho-Anal.*, 94:501–530.

Bowlby, J. (1969). *Attachment and loss, vol. 1: Attachment.* New York, NY: Basic Books.

Bowlby, J. (1973). *Attachment and loss, vol. 2: Separation, anxiety and mourning.* New York: Basic Books.

Bowlby, J. (1989). The role of attachment in personality development and psycho-pathology. In S. I. Greenspan, G. H. Pollock (Eds.), *The course of life, Vol. 1: Infancy* (pp. 229–270). Madison, CT, US: International Universities Press, Inc.

Brenner, C. (1976). Psychic conflict and the analyst's task. In *Psychoanalytic technique and psychic conflict* (8–34). New York: International Universities Press.

Briere, J. and Elliot, D.M. (2003). Prevalence and psychological sequelae of self-reported childhood physical and sexual abuse in a general population sample of men and women. Child Abuse & Neglect Elsevier Science. 1205–1222.

Britton, J.C., Lissek, S., Grillon, C., Norcross, M.A., Pine, D.S. (2011) Development of anxiety: the role of threat appraisal and fear learning. *Depression and Anxiety.* 28(1):5–17.

Busch F. Our vital profession. *Int J Psychoanal.* 2015 Jun; 96(3):553–68.

Cabaniss, D. L. (2010). *Psychodynamic psychotherapy: A clinical manual.* Oxford: Wiley-Blackwell.

Carlson, V., Cicchetti, D., Barnett, D., Braunwald, K. (1989). Disorganized/disoriented attachment relationships in maltreated infants. *Developmental Psychology*, 25(4), 525–531.

Chefetz, R. A. (2015). *Intensive psychotherapy for persistent dissociative processes: The fear of feeling real.* New York: Norton.

Christian, C., Safran, J. D., & Muran, J. C. (2012). The corrective emotional experience: A relational perspective and critique. In L. G. Castonguay, C. E. Hill (Eds.), *Transformation in psychotherapy: Corrective experiences across cognitive behavioral, humanistic, and psychodynamic approaches* (51–67). Washington, DC, US: American Psychological Association.

Clarkin, J.F., Yeomans, F.E., Kernberg, O.F. (2006). *Psychotherapy for borderline personality: Focusing on object relations.* Arlington, VA: American Psychiatric Pub Inc.

Conte, H. R. & Plutchik, R. (1995). *Ego defenses: Theory and measurement.* New York, NY: Wiley.

Crits-Christoph, P., Demorest, A., & Connolly, M. B. (1990). Quantitative assessment of interpersonal themes over the course of a psychotherapy. Psychotherapy, 27, 513–521.

Crits-Christoph, P., & Demorest, A. (1991). Qualitative assessment of relationship theme components. In M. J. Horowitz, ed., *Person schemas and maladaptive interpersonal patterns.* Chicago: University of Chicago Press.

Curtis, R.C. (2012). New experiences and meanings: A Model of change for Psychoanalysis. *Psychoanalytic Psychology*, 29:81–98.

Emde, R. N. and J. F. Sorce. (1983). *Rewards of infancy: Emotional availability and maternal referencing.* In J. Coll, E. Galenson, & R. Tyson, (Eds.), *Frontiers of Infant Psychiatry.* New York: Basic Books.

Fairbairn, W.R.D. (1943). The repression and return of bad objects (with special reference to war neuroses). In W.R.D. Fairbairn (Ed.), *Psychoanalytic studies of the personality* (78–97). New York, NY: Routledge.

Fairbairn, W.R.D. (1944) Endopsychic structure considered in terms of object-relationships. In W.R.D. Fairbairn (Ed.), *Psychoanalytic studies of the personality* (98–137). New York, NY: Routledge.

Farber, S.K. (2008). Dissociation, traumatic attachments, and self-harm: Eating disorders and self-mutilation. *Clinical Social Work Journal, 36*, 63–72.

Ferro, A., (2011). *Avoiding emotions, living emotions*. Hove, East Sussex: Routledge.

Fonagy, P. & Bateman, A. W. (2005). Attachment Theory and Mentalization-Oriented Model of Borderline Personality Disorder. In J. M. Oldham, A. E. Skodol, D. S. Bender (Eds.), *The American Psychiatric Publishing textbook of personality disorders* (pp. 187–207). Arlington, VA, US: American Psychiatric Publishing, Inc.

Fonagy, P. & Target, M. (2000). Playing with reality III: The persistence of dual psychic reality in borderline patients. *International Journal of Psychoanalysis, 81* (5), 853–874.

Fonagy, P. & Target, M. (2006). The mentalization-focused approach to self pathology. *Journal of Personality Disorders, 20*(6), 544–576.

Fonagy, P., Gergely, G., Jurist, E. L., & Target, M. (2004). *Affect regulation, mentalization, and the development of the self*. New York, NY: Other Press.

Fonagy, P., Steele, H., & Steele M. (1991). Maternal representations of attachment during pregnancy predict the organization of infant-mother attachment at one year of age. *Child Development*. 62, 891–905.

Freud, A. & Baines, C. (1996). *The ego and the mechanisms of defense*. International University Press.

Freud, S. (1912). *Recommendation to physicians practicing psychoanalysis*. London: Hogarth Press.

Freud, S. & Strachey, J. (1977). *Introductory lectures on psychoanalysis*. New York: Norton.

Frijda, N. H. (1986). *The emotions*. Cambridge, England: Cambridge University Press.

Frijda, N. H., Kuipers, P., & ter Schure, E. (1989). Relations among emotion, appraisal, and emotional action readiness. *Journal of Personality and Social Psychology, 57*, 212–228.

Gabbard, G. O. (2014). *Psychodynamic psychiatry in clinical practice*. American Psychiatric Publishing.

Gedo, J. E. and Goldberg, A. (1975). *Models of the mind. A psychoanalytic theory*. The University of Chicago Press.

Goffman, E. (1974). *Frame analysis*. New York: Harper.

Goldfried, M. R. & Davila, J. (2005). The role of relationship and technique in therapeutic change. *Psychotherapy theory, research, practice, training*, 42, 421–430.

Greenberg, J.R. (1986). The problem of analytic neutrality. *Contemporary Psychoanalysis, 22*, 76–86.

Greenberg, L. (2008). Emotion and cognition in psychotherapy: The transforming power of affect. *Canadian psychology, 49*(1), 49–59.

Grienenberger, J.F., Kelly, K., Slade, A. (2005). Maternal reflective functioning, mother-infant affective communication, and infant attachment. *Attachment and Human Development, 7*(3), 299–311.

Gunderson, J. G. (2009). Borderline Personality Disorder: Ontogeny of a Diagnosis. *The American Journal of Psychiatry, 166*(5), 530–539. doi:10.1176/appi.ajp.2009.08121825.

Herman, J. L. (1997). *Trauma and recovery*. New York: Basic Books.

Herman, J. L. & Hirschman, L. (2000). *Father-daughter incest*. Cambridge, MA: Harvard University Press.

Herman, J.L. (2008). Craft and science in the treatment of traumatized people. *J Trauma Dissociation*. 9(3):293–300.

Hesse, E., Main, M. (2000). Disorganized infant, child, and adult attachment. *Journal of American Psychoanalytical Association, 48*, 1097–1127.

Høglend, P., Hersoug, A.G., Bøgwald, K.P., Amlo, S., Marble, A., Sørbye, Ø., Røssberg, J.I., Ulberg, R., Gabbard, G.O., Crits-Christoph, P. (2011). Effects of transference work in the context of therapeutic alliance and quality of object relations. *J Consult Clin Psychol.*

Høglend P. (2014). Exploration of the patient-therapist relationship in psychotherapy. *Am J Psychiatry.* 171(10):1056–66.

Holmes, D.S. (1974). Investigations of repression: Differential recall of material experimentally or naturally associated with ego threat. *Psychological bulletin,* 81:632–653.

Holmes, J. (1997). Attachment, autonomy, intimacy: Some clinical implications of attachment theory. *British Journal of Medical Psychology,* 70: 231–248.

Horowitz, M.J. (2014). *Identity and the new psychoanalytic explorations of self-organization.* London: Routledge.

Horowitz, M.J. (2013). *Disturbed personality functioning and psychotherapy technique Psychotherapy:* 50: 438–442.

Horowitz, M. J. (2014). Clarifying values in psychotherapy. *Psychodyn Psychiatry, 42*(4), 671–679.

Horowitz, M.J., Wilner, N., Marmar, C., Krupnick, J. Pathological grief and the activation of latent self-images. *Am J Psychiatry.* 1980 Oct; 137(10):1157–2.

Horowitz, M.J., Understanding and ameliorating revenge fantasies in psychotherapy. *Am J Psychiatry.* 2007 Jan; 164(1):24–7.

Horowitz, M. J. (1979). *States of mind: Analysis of change in psychotherapy.* New York, NY: Plenum Medical Book Co.

Horowitz, M. J. (1986). Levels of interpretation in dynamic psychotherapy. *Psychoanalytic Psychology, 3*, 39–45.

Horowitz, M. J. (1988b). *Introduction to psychodynamics: A new synthesis.* New York, NY: Basic Books.

Horowitz, M. J. (1991). *Person schemas and maladaptive interpersonal patterns.* Chicago, IL: University of Chicago Press.

Horowitz, M. J. (1997). *Personality styles and brief psychotherapy.* Northvale, N.J: J. Aronson.

Horowitz, M. J. (2005). *Understanding psychotherapy change: A practical guide to configurational analysis.* Washington, DC: American Psychological Association.

Horowitz, M. J. (2011). *Stress response syndromes (5th ed.).* Northvale, NJ: Jason Aronson.

Horowitz, M. J. (Ed.). (1988a). *Psychodynamics and cognition.* Chicago, IL: University of Chicago Press.

Horowitz, M. J. & Stinson, C. H. (1995). Defenses as aspects of person schemas and control processes. In H. Conte & R. Plutchik (Eds.), *Ego defenses: Theory and measurement* (pp. 79–97). NY: Wiley.

Horowitz, M. J., Cooper, S., Fridhandler, B., Perry, J. C., Bond, M., & Vaillant, G. (1992). Control processes and defense mechanisms. *Journal of Psychotherapy Practice and Research*, 1(4), 324–336.

Horowitz, M. J., Cooper, S., Fridhandler, B., Perry, J. D., Bond, M., & Vaillant, G. E. (1992). Control processes and defense mechanisms. *Journal of Psychotherapy Practice and Research* 1:324–336.

Horowitz, M. J., Markman, H. C., Stinson, C. H., Ghannam, J. H., & Fridhandler, B. A. (1990). Classification theory of defense. In J. Singer (Ed.), *Repression and dissociation: Implications for personality theory, psychopathology and health* (pp. 61–84). Chicago, IL: University of Chicago Press.

Horowitz, M. J., Marmar, C., Krupnick, J., Wilner, N., Kaltreider, N., Wallerstein, R. (2001). *Personality styles and brief psychotherapy.* J. Aronson.

Horowitz, M. J., Milbrath, C., Jordan, D. S., Stinson, C. H., Ewert, M., Redington, D. J., Fridhandler, B., Reidbord, S. P. and Hartley, D. (1994). Expressive and defensive behavior during discourse on unresolved topics: A single case study of pathological grief. *Journal of Personality*, 62: 527–563.

Horowitz, M. J., Znoj, H., & Stinson, C. (1996). Defensive control processes: Use of theory in research, formulation, and therapy of stress response syndromes. In M. Zeidner & N. Endler (Eds.), *Handbook of coping* (pp. 532–553). New York, NY: Wiley and Sons.

Horowitz, M.J. (1995). *Defensive control of states and person schemas.* pp. 67–90 in Shapiro, T., & Emde, R. N. (1995), *Research in psychoanalysis: Process, development, outcome.* Madison, CT: International Universities Press.

Horowitz, M., Cooper, S., Fridhandler, B., Perry, J. C., Bond, M., & Vaillant, G. (1992). Control processes and defense mechanisms. *The Journal of Psychotherapy Practice and Research*, 1(4), 324–336.

Horowitz, M.J. (1988). *Introduction to psychodynamics: A new synthesis.* New York: Basic Books.

Horowitz, M.J. (1998). *Cognitive psychodynamics: From conflict to character.* New York, NY: Wiley.

Horowitz, M.J. (2009) *A course in happiness.* NY: Penguin Group.

Horowitz, M.J. (2011). *Stress response syndromes*, 5th ed. NJ: Aronson.

Horowitz, M.J., Marmar, C., Krupnick, J., Wilner, N., Kaltreider, N., & Wallerstein, R.S. (1997). *Personality styles and brief psychotherapy.* Northvale, NJ: Jason Aronson.

Horowitz, M.J., Möller B. (2009). Formulating transference in cognitive and dynamic psychotherapies using role relationship models. *J Psychiatr Pract.* 15(1):25–33.

Huprich, S. K. (2014). Malignant self-regard: A self-structure enhancing the understanding of masochistic, depressive, and vulnerably narcissistic personalities. *Harvard Review of Psychiatry, 22*, 295–305.

Jacobson, E. (1964). *The self in the object world.* New York: International Universities Press.

Kealy, D., Ogrodnikzuk, J. (2014). Pathological narcissism and the obstruction of love. *Psychodynamic Psychiatry.* 42(1): 101–119.

Kernberg, O.F. (2014). An overview of the treatment of severe narcissistic pathology. *Int J Psychoanal.*

Kernberg, O.F. (1980). *Internal world and external reality: Object relations theory applied.* New York: Jason Aronson.

Klein, G.S. (1976). *Psychoanalytic theory.* New York: International Universities Press.

Klein, M. (1940). Mourning and its relation to manic-depressive states. *Int. J. Psycho-Anal.*, 21:125–153.

Knapp, P.H. (1991). Selfother schemas: Core organizers of human experience. M.J. Horowitz, ed., *Person schemas and maladaptive interpersonal patterns.* Chicago: University of Chicago Press.

Kohut H. (1977). *The restoration of the self.* New York: International Universities Press.

Kohut, H. (1972) *Analysis of the Self.* Norton.

Kohut, H. (1972). Thoughts on narcissism and narcissistic rage. *Psychoanalytic Study of the Child* 27:360–400.

Kohut, H. (1984). How does analysis cure? In A. Goldberg and P. Stepansky, eds., *Contributions to the psychology of the self*. Chicago: University of Chicago Press.

Krupnick, J.L. & Melnikoff, S.E. (2012). Psychotherapy with low-income patients. *Contemporary Psychotherapy*, Special Issue, 42(1):7–15.

LeDoux, J. E. (1995). Emotions: Clues from the brain. *Annual Review of Psychology, 46*, 209–235.

Levenson, H., & American Psychological Association. (2010). *Brief dynamic therapy*. Washington, DC: American Psychological Association.

Levy, K. N., & Anderson, T. (2013). Is clinical psychology doctoral training becoming less intellectually diverse? And if so, what can be done? *Clinical Psychology: Science and Practice*, 20(2), 211–220.

Levy, K. N., Ellison, W. D., Scott, L. N., & Bernecker, S. L. (2011). Attachment style. *Journal of Clinical Psychology, 67*(2), 193–201.

Lingiardi, V., McWilliams N., Bornstein, R. F., Gazzillo, F., & Gordon, R. (2015). The Psychodynamic Diagnostic Manual version 2 (PDM-2): Assessing patients for improved clinical practice and research. *Psychoanalytic Psychology, 32*, 94–115.

Loftus, E.F. (1997) Creating false memories. *Sci Am.* 277(3):70–5.

Luborsky, L. (1984). *Principles of psychoanalytic psychotherapy: A manual for supportive-expressive (SE) treatment*. New York: Basic Books.

Luyten, P., & Blatt, S. J. (2013). Interpersonal relatedness and self-definition in normal and disrupted personality development: Retrospect and prospect. *American Psychologist, 68*, 172–183.

Lyons-Ruth, K. (1996). Attachment relationships among children with aggressive behavior problems. *Journal of Clinical and Consulting Psychology*, 64–73.

Marmar, R., Horowitz, M. J. (1986). Phenomenological analysis of splitting. *Psychotherapy: Theory, Research, Practice, Training*, Vol 23(1), 1986, 21–29.

McClelland, J. L., Rumelhart, D. E., & the PDP Research Group. (1986). *Parallel distributed processing: Explorations in the microstructure of cognition. Volume II*. Cambridge, MA: MIT Press.

McWilliams, N. (2011). *Psychoanalytic diagnosis: Understanding personality structure in the clinical process*, rev. ed. New York: Guilford Press.

Millon, T. & Davis, R. D. (1996). *Disorders of personality: DSM-IV and beyond*. New York: Wiley.

Milrod, B. (1997). *Manual of panic-focused psychodynamic psychotherapy*. Washington, DC: American Psychiatric Press.

Milrod, B., Markowitz, J. C., Gerber, A. J., Cyranowski, J., Altemus, M., Shapiro, T., & Glatt, C. (2014). Childhood separation anxiety and the pathogenesis and treatment of adult anxiety. *The American Journal of Psychiatry*, 171(1), 34–43.

Modell AH. (1976). "The Holding Environment" and the therapeutic action of psychoanalysis. *J Am Psychoanal Assoc*. 1976; 24(2):285–307.

Music, G. (2011). *Nurturing natures: Attachment and children's emotional, sociocultural and brain development*. New York, NY: Psychology Press.

Norcross, J.C., Wampold, B.E. (2011). Evidence-based therapy relationships: Research conclusions and clinical practices. *Psychotherapy*, 48 (1), pp. 98–102.

Olson, T.R., Perry, J.C., Janzen, J.I., Petraglia, J., Presniak, M.D. (2011). Addressing and interpreting defense mechanisms in psychotherapy: general considerations. *Psychiatry*. 74(2):142–65.

Panksepp, J., & Biven, L. (2012). *The archeology of mind: Neuroevolutionary origins of human emotions*. New York: Norton.

Perry, J. C. (2014). Anomalies and specific functions in the clinical identification of defense mechanisms. *Journal of Clinical Psychology, 70,* 406˜418.

Perry, J. C., Augusto, F., & Cooper, S. H. (1989). Assessing psychodynamic conflicts: I. Reliability of the idiographic conflict formulation method. *Psychiatry, 52,* 289301.

Persons, J. B. (1989). *Cognitive therapy in practice: A case formulation approach.* New York, NY; London: W.W. Norton & Company.

Persons, J. B. (1992). A case formulation approach to cognitive-behavior therapy: Application to panic disorder. *Psychiatric Annals, 22*(9), 470–473.

Pine, F. (1985). *Developmental theory and clinical process.* New Haven and London: Yale University Press.

Piper, W. and Duncan, S. (1999) Object relationship theory and short-term dynamic psychotherapy. *Clinical Psychology Review,* 19:669–685.

Porges, S. W. (2011). *The polyvagal theory. Neurophysiological foundations of emotions, attachment, communication and self-regulation.* New York: Norton.

Reidbord, S.P., Redington, D. J. (1993). Nonlinear analysis of autonomic responses in a therapist during psychotherapy. *Journal of Nervous & Mental Disease.* 181(7):428–435.

Renick, O. (2006). *Practical psychoanalysis for therapists and patients.* New York: Other Press.

Rice T.R., Hoffman L. (2014). Defense mechanisms and implicit emotion regulation: a comparison of a psychodynamic construct with one from contemporary neuroscience. *J Am Psychoanal Assoc.* 62(4):693–708.

Rogers, C. (1951). *Client-centered therapy.* Oxford, England: Houghton Mifflin.

Rogers, C. R. (1957). The necessary and sufficient conditions of therapeutic personality change. *Journal of Consulting Psychology, 21*(2), 95–103.

Rumelhart, D. E., McClelland, J. L., & the PDP Research Group. (1986). *Parallel distributed processing: Explorations in the microstructure of cognition. Volume I.* Cambridge, MA: MIT Press.

Saklofske, D. H., & Zeidner, M. (1995). *Personality and intelligence.* New York, NY: Springer Publishing Company.

Sandler, C.M. (1960). The background of safety. *International Journal of Psychoanalysis* 41, 352–356.

Schafer, R. (1983). *The analytic attitude.* New York: Basic Books, Inc.

Scherer, K.R. (1988) 'Criteria for Emotion-Antecedent Appraisal: A Review', in V. Hamilton, G.H. Bower and N.H. Frijda (eds), *Cognitive Perspectives on Emotion and Motivation,* pp. 89–126.

Scherer, K.R. (1999). Appraisal theory. In T. Dalgleish & M. Power (Eds.), *Handbook of Cognition and Emotion.* New York: Wiley.

Shapiro, D. (1965). *Neurotic styles.* New York, NY: Basic Books.

Shapiro, D. (1981). *Autonomy and rigid character.* New York, NY: Basic Books.

Shapiro, D. (2000). *Dynamics of character.* New York, NY: Basic Books.

Shedler, J. (2015). Integrating clinical and empirical perspectives on personality: The Shedler-Westen Assessment Procedure (SWAP). In S. K. Huprich (Ed.), *Personality disorders: Toward theoretical and empirical integration.*

Singer, J. L. (Ed.). (1990). *Repression and dissociation: Implications for personality theory, psychopathology, and health.* Chicago, IL: University of Chicago Press.

Singer, J.L. (1987). Private experience and public action: The study of ongoing conscious thought. In J. Aronoff, A. Rabin and R.A. Zucker, eds., *The emergence of personality.* New York: Springer.

Skolnikoff, A. (2009). The emotional position of the analyst in the shift from psychotherapy to psychoanalysis. Psychoanalytic Inquiry.

Smith, C.A. & Lazarus, R.S. (1993). Appraisal components, core relational themes, and the emotions. *Cognition and Emotion, 7*, 233–269.

Smith, E. R., & Mackie, D. M. (2008). Intergroup emotions. In M. Lewis, J. Haviland-Jones, and L. F. Barrett (Eds.), *Handbook of Emotions* (3rd Edition, pp. 428–439). New York: Guilford Publications.

Sroufe, L.A. (1979). The coherence of individual development: Early care, attachment, and subsequent developmental issues. *American Psychologist, 34*(10), 834–841.

Sroufe, L.A. (1996). *Emotional development: The organization of emotional life in the early years.* New York: Cambridge University Press.

Stayton, D. J., & Ainsworth, M. D. (1973). Individual differences in infant responses to brief, everyday separations as related to other infant and maternal behaviors. *Developmental Psychology, 9*(2), 226–235.

Steele, H., & Steele, M. (2008). On the origins of reflective functioning. In F. Busch (Ed), *Mentalization: Theoretical considerations, research findings, and clinical implications. Psychoanalytic Inquiry Book Series, 29*, pp. 133–158. NY: Analytic Books.

Stern D. N: (1998). The process of therapeutic change involving implicit knowledge: Some implications of developmental observations for adult psychotherapy. *Infant Mental Health Journal. Special Issue: Interventions that affect change in psychotherapy: A model based on infant research.* 19(3), 300–308.

Stern, D. N. (2004) *The present moment: In psychotherapy and everyday life.* Norton Series on Interpersonal Neurobiology. New York, NY: W. W. Norton & Co.

Stern, D.N. (1985). *The interpersonal world of the infant.* New York, NY: Basic Books.

Stoller, R. (1968). *Sex and gender, vol. 1: The transsexual experiment.* New York: Aronson.

Stolorow, R. D., & Lachmann, F. M. (1980). *The psychoanalysis of developmental arrests.* New York: International Universities Press.

Tronick, E.Z. (2007). *The neurobehavioral and social-emotional development of infants and children.* New York: W.W. Norton & Co. Wallerstein, R.S. (1986). *Forty-two lives in treatment: a study of psychoanalysis and psychotherapy.* New York: Guilford Press.

United States Administration for Children and Families. (2005). Child maltreatment 2003: Reports from the states to the National Child Abuse and Neglect Data Systems – national statistics on child abuse and neglect.

Vaillant, G. E. (1994). Ego mechanisms of defense and personality psychopathology. *Journal of Abnormal Psychology, 102*(1), 44–50.

Vaillant, G. E. (2003). *Aging well: Guideposts to a happier life.* New York: Warner.

Wachtel, P. (2014). An Integrative Relational Points of View. *Psychotherapy, 51*, 342–349.

Wachtel, P. L. (2011). *Inside the session: What really happens in psychotherapy.* Washington, DC: American Psychological Association.

Wacthel, P.L. (1993). *Therapeutic communication: Knowing what to say when.* New York, NY: The Guilford Press.

Weiss, J., & Sampson, H. (Eds.) (1986). *The psychoanalytic process: Theory, clinical observation and empirical research.* New York: Guilford Press.

Westen, D., Shedler, J., Bradley, B., & DeFife, J. A. (2012). An empirically derived taxonomy for personality diagnosis: Bridging science and practice in conceptualizing personality. *American Journal of Psychiatry, 169*, 273–284.

Whalen, P. J., Rauch, S. L., Etcoff, N. L., McInerny, S., Lee, M. B., & Jenike, M. A. (1998). Masked presentations of emotional facial expressions modulate amygdala activity without explicit knowledge. *Journal of Neuroscience, 18*, 411–418.

Winnicott, D.W. (1965). *The maturational processes and the facilitating environment: Studies in the theory of emotional development.* New York: International Universities Press.

Winnicott, D.W. (1972). Mirror-role of mother and family in child development. *Playing and reality* (pp. 111–119). London: Tavistock Publications.

Winnicott, D.W. (1989). *Psychoanalytic exploration.* Harvard University Press, Cambridge.

Young, J. E. (1994). *Cognitive therapy for personality disorders: A schema-focused approach* (3rd ed.). Sarasota, FL: Professional Resource Exchange, Incorporated.

Young, J. E., Klosko, J. S., & Weishaar, M. E. (2006). *Schema therapy: A practitioner's guide.* New York: Guilford Press.

Zimmermann, J., Ehrenthal, J. C., Cierpka, M., Schauenburg, H., Doering, S., & Benecke, C. (2012). Assessing the level of structural integration using Operationalized Psychodynamic Diagnosis (OPD): Implications for DSM–5. *Journal of Personality Assessment*, 94, 522–532.

Glossary of terms

This glossary is from the book *Adult Personality Growth in Psychotherapy* by Mardi Horowitz, M.D.

Belief structure: The associational pattern that connects elements of information into a meaningful complex.

Character: Learned, enduring, but only slowly changing attitudes and cognitive maps that lend continuity over time to a sense of identity and constancy in attachments.

Configuration: A set of associatively related beliefs. Harmonious configurations have well-integrated elements. Conflictual configurations have poorly integrated elements, which may have associated identity disturbances.

Configurational analysis: A system of formulation that describes: (1) phenomena to be explained, (2) states in which the phenomena do and do not occur, (3) themes that lead to state changes and defensive controls that are used to regulate the emotions of these themes, and (4) configurations of self-other attitudes.

Cycles: Repeated, sequential patterns.

Declarative knowledge: Beliefs that are consciously represented and can be communicated.

Emotional-control processes: Mental activities, often operating unconsciously, that ward off dreaded states (e.g., anxiety, terror, rage, or depression). These regulatory processes use inhibitions and facilitations, which can affect both form and content of thought, as well as schemas used to organize thinking, feeling, planning, and acting.

Identity: Awareness of the self as a continuous, and usually, coherent entity that perceives, thinks, feels, decides, and acts. Conscious identity rests upon belief structures of one's unconscious self-organization.

Insight: A realization about the cause and/or effect of a situation or a conscious connection between elements in a pattern.

Integrated attention: The result of putting together, or the blending, of meanings that allows a person to navigate easily between various modes of representation; for example, when one translates visual images into words.

Magical thinking: Arriving at assumptions based in fantasy rather than the realistic appraisals of a situation.

Motives: The reasons for decisions. There may be motives to enact, as well as motives to restrain action. There may be motives to think consciously or not to think consciously about a particular topic, memory, or unconscious fantasy. Motives usually refer to enduring themes in self-organization, whereas the word *intention* is used to refer to more transient aims.

Parallel processing: The simultaneous processing of information in relatively separate channels. For example, a person might appraise a current danger situation and plan intentions by emotional cognitive processing organized by (1) a competent self-schema, and (2) an incompetent self-schema. Parallel processing can yield divergent conclusions.

Person schema: The self or other persons regarded as an organized whole including body images, traits, roles, values, and mannerisms. The subordinate parts of a person schema are beliefs, nesting in a hierarchy leading up to the whole. Less than the organized whole, there can be fragmentary self-schemas.

Personality: An individual's enduring and slowly changing configurations of beliefs, preferences, values, traits, and tendencies that make up a unique combining potential moods, thoughts, and behaviors. Personality consists of the important components of identity and one's relationship patterns, as well as that person's capacities for emotional regulation.

Preconscious processing: Preparatory mental manipulation of information that occurs before conscious representation. Parallel processing may proceed using different role-relationship models as organizers of information.

Procedural knowledge: "Know-how" that can lead to automatic action sequences without the concomitant "declaration" of such knowledge in reflective consciousness, operating either preconsciously or unconsciously.

Projection: A defensive operation in which an attribute of the self is externalized and regarded as coming from or motivating another person's perceived emotions, words, and actions.

Psychodynamic configuration: A constellation of motives, defined at the psychological level in terms of wishes, fears, and defensive strategies. A configuration of conflict usually involves a wishfully impulsive aim—a threat that is viewed as a possible consequence of impulsive action toward a desired goal, and a defensive posture that, though compromising the wish, avoids the feared consequences.

Relational model: A descriptive, generalized, cognitive map of the roles, transactions, aims, and senses of connection between self and others.

Representations: Iconic or symbolically encoded meanings that are capable of either conscious awareness or communicative expression. Representations occur in modes such as images, lexical (verbal) propositions, or enactive (somatic) propositions.

Reschematization: The process of altering belief structures by adding new elements, reorganizing prior elements, and altering linkage-strength patterns in the associational connection between elements. The result can modify personality-based attitudes and assumptions.

Role-relationship models (RRMs): Inner schemas and scripts blueprinting interpersonal transactions, as well as attributes of self and others. Some RRMs are *desired*: they depict positive outcomes that a person seeks to achieve. Other RRMs are *dreaded*: they depict negative outcomes that a person seeks to avoid. In addition, some RRMs are compromises, used to avoid wish-fear dilemmas. Of these, there are *problematic compromises*, containing symptom-causing elements, and *protective compromises*, containing coping or defensive elements.

Schema: A usually unconscious meaning that can serve as an organizer in the formation of thought. Schemas influence how motives reach awareness and action. Schemas tend to endure, and they change slowly, as the integration of new understandings modify earlier forms. Small-order schemas can be nested into hierarchies, together acting as larger order or supra-ordinate schemas.

Self-concept: The recurrent belief of self-attribution that can be—and at least once, has been—consciously represented.

Self-objects: Other people or things that an individual views as an extension of him- or herself, rather than a fully separate and autonomous thing or person.

Self-organization: A person's overall set of available schemas and supra-ordinate schemas.

Self-reflective awareness: A state in which self-observation is incorporated into awareness or sensory streams.

Self-schema: One of several potentials in cognitive maps that can when activated serve as an unconscious organizer of many features of the individual into a holistic pattern of thought, mood, and behavior.

Self-state: A temporary constellation of feelings and definitions of identity emerging from the activation of self-schemas and acting as the current organizer of connections between sets of information, while interacting with current sensory inputs, including how the self is perceived as being reflected by significant others.

States of mind: Combinations of conscious and unconscious experiences, with patterns of behavior that last for a period of time and that can be observed by others as having emotional, regulatory, or motivational qualities.

Supraordinate self-schema: A larger structure that contains a configuration of multiple, subordinate self-schemas.

Therapeutic alliance: The relationship that forms between a patient and a therapist, which allows them to work together toward a mutual goal.

Transference: The displacement of ideas, feelings, motives, and actions associated with a previous relationship to a current relationship, to a degree that the belief structure is, at least in part, inappropriate. *Counter-transference* by a therapist classically involves reactive feelings elicited by the patient's transference toward the therapist. However, commonly, clinicians use the term counter-transference to refer to feelings that the therapist feels toward the patient, regardless of whether or not those feelings are brought on by the patient's transference, or by the therapist's own transference toward the patient.

Working model: The currently active schematic organization of beliefs. A working model usually combines perceived information with information from activated, enduring schemas.

Index

abandonment fears, excessive, 55–56
accusation, 77
active memory, 93
ambivalent transference feelings, 72
ambivalent/resistant attachment style,
    21–22
anxiety, 1–2, 34
    separation, 21–22, 24–25, 30, 38
    stranger, 21
apathetic state of mind, 4
associations, linked, 92–93
attachment, 21
    in childhood, 55
    passivity as strategy for, 56
    styles of, 21–22
attention
    excessive seeking of, 57
    focusing on topic, 8–9, 95–96
    integrated, 134–135
    negative attentional bias, 42
    sulking and, 45–46
    topics deserving more, 38–39
Augusto, F., 117–118
automatic responses, 69
avoidances, 5–6, 16, 29, 32–33, 38, 69–70,
    106. See also emotional avoidance
    maneuvers
    patterns of, 8–9
    of shame, 94–96
avoidant attachment style, 21–22
avoidant behaviors, 107
avoidant relationship patterns, 58

Beck, A., 42
belief structure, 134
best-case scenarios, 8
Beuchler, S., 8
Bion, W. R., 10
blame, 77
blind spots, 8–9
bodily reactions, 65–66
borderline personality disorders, 99–100

cause-and-effect
    scenarios, 31
    sequences, 8, 32–33
character, 134
childhood, 21–23, 66
    attachment in, 55
    paranoid position and, 42
    self-narratives and, 37, 42–43
    sexual abuse in, 78–79, 80
    stress and, 66–67
    trauma in, 41
    unconscious attitudes of, 42–43
child-parent role models, 54
clarification, of patterns, 24–25, 43–44, 69–70
cognitive distortion, 106
cognitive maps, 17–18, 40, 54
cognitive processing, 31–32
competition, 57
compliance, 40–41
compromise, 20–21
compulsive patterns, of defensive styles, 99–100
compulsive repetitions, 69
configuration, 134
    psychodynamic, 135–136
    of scenarios, 30–31
    supraordinate, 17
configurational analysis, 3–4, 134
confrontation, 67
connectivity, enhancing, 25–26
conscious awareness, 9–10
    reflective, 34
conscious reflection, 40
conscious representations, 115
conscious thought, 11
Conte, H. R., 117–118
Cooper, S. H., 117–118
cooperative partnerships, 2
corrective experiences, 10–11
counter-transference, 10–11, 31, 65–66, 136
critical role, 69–70
cycles, 134
    state and relationship, 30

declarative knowledge, 134
declarative statements, 6
defensive RRMs, 55–56
defensive styles, 9–10, 99
    avoidant behaviors and, 107
    conclusion to, 108
    formulation and, 103
        projection, 104–106
    observation and, 99–100
        disavowal, 101
        displacement, 101
        dissociation, 102–103
        idealization, 101
        intellectualization, 100
        projection, 103
        rationalization, 100
        reaction formation, 100–101
        repression, 102
        role reversal, 103
        splitting, 102–103
        undoing, 101–102
    techniques and, 106–108
degraded self-concept, 57–58
degraded self-schemas, 34–35
demoralization, 81–82
denial, 101
depersonalization, 19
depression, 81
depressive position, 42
derealization, 19
desire, sexual, 78
desired RRMs, 135–136
desired scenarios, 17–18
developmental psychology, 78
Diagnostic and Statistical Manual
        (5th edition), 19–20
dilemmas, 73, 83–84
    sample, 74
    wish-fear, 20–21, 30–31, 34, 47–48, 55–56,
        122–123
direct guidance, 67–68
disavowal, 101
disorganized/disoriented attachment style, 21–22
displacement, 101
dissociation, 16, 17, 25, 40–41
    defensive styles and, 102–103
    self-states and, 41
dissociative processes, 32
dormant RRMs, 54
dreaded responses, 73–75
dreaded RRMs, 135–136
dreaded scenarios, 17–18
dysfunctional beliefs, 31

emotion, 63–64, 91. *See also* unconscious
        emotional potentials
    containment of, 7–8
    expression of, 32–35, 91
    regulation of, 4, 92, 110–112
    shifts of, 66–67
emotional attitudes, 10–11
emotional avoidance maneuvers, 109
    formulation and, 113–118
    observation and, 109–113
    outcomes of, 111, 112, 114, 115, 116, 117
    summary of, 124
    technique and, 118–124
emotional states, 16
emotional-control processes, 8–9,
        134–135
emotionality, 99
empathy, 10–11, 19, 21–22, 65, 86–87
episodic memory, 69
erotic transference, 81–84
excessive attention seeking, 57
excessive emotional reactions, 37–38
excessive fear of abandonment, 55–56
exhibitionism, 80
explicit statements, 6
exploratory psychotherapy, 65, 70
extreme trains of thought, 96–97

false self, 30–31, 41
fear. *See also* anxiety
    of abandonment, 22–23, 55–56, 58–59
    wish-fear dilemma, 20–21, 30–31, 34, 47–48,
        55–56, 122–123
forgiveness, 73–75, 86–87
Freud, Sigmund, 7–8

Gedo, J. E., 73
gender preferences, 77
general capacities, deficiencies in, 1–2
general technique principles, 7
    emotional attitudes, 10–11
    emotional containment, 7–8
    evaluating progress, 9–10
    focusing attention on topic, 8–9
    safety, 7–8
generalization, 100
Generalized Anxiety Disorder, 2
Goldberg, A., 73
good-enough parenting, 21–22
Great Depression, 96–97
Greenberg, J. R., 8
Greinenberger, J. F., 22
gut-level sensations, 27–28

habitual beliefs, 6
happiness, 4
harsh inner critics, 57–58
helper role, 69–70
here-and-now middle ground, 72–73
histrionic patterns, of defensive styles, 99–100
Histrionic Personality Disorder, 81
holding environment, 73
hoped-for responses, 73–75
Horowitz, M. J., 117–118
hyper-vigilance, 44, 58

ideal imagined future, 97
idealization, 101
identity, 13, 19, 134–135
    coherent, 1
    gender preferences and, 77
    narratives, 40–41
    sexual preferences and, 77
in-between responses, 73–75
indecisiveness, 101–102
infancy, 21–22, 42–43
inner critics, harsh, 57–58
inner motives, 30
insight, 11, 43–44, 46–48, 49–50, 69, 134–135
integrated attention, 134–135
integration, levels of, 18–19, 26
intellectualization, 100, 120–121
interpersonal patterns, 3
intimacy, 19
intrusive ideas and feelings, 37–38
irritation, 38–39

Kelly, K., 22
Klein, Melanie, 42
Kohut, H., 42, 73

levels of integration, 18–19, 26
linked associations, 92–93
linking, 45
loneliness, 81
love-hate thinking, 72–73

macro-formulations, 3
magical thinking, 134–135
Major Depressive Disorder, 81
Markman, H. C., 117–118
meaning structures, 17–18
memory, 70–72
    active, 93
    episodic, 69
    of trauma, 92–93
    working, 32

mental health advice, 23
mentalization, 10
middle ground, 70–73
misappraisals, 24–25
misinterpretations, 23–24
Modell, A. H., 73
moral restraint, 84
most likely scenarios, 8
motives, 134–135
mutuality, 65

narcissism, 60–62
narcissistic patterns, of defensive styles, 99–100
Narcissistic Personality Disorder, 2
negative attentional bias, 42
neutrality, 7–8
non-critical stance, 55

Organizational Levels of Self and Other
        Schematization, 19
over-control, 92, 93–94
over-modulated states of mind, 4, 27, 28, 53–54

parallel processing, 24–25, 46, 134–135
    self-narratives and, 48–49
paranoid position, 42
parental reflective functioning, 22
passive-aggressive relationship patterns, 59–60
passivity, 40–41
    as attachment strategy, 56
pathological self-soothing, 57
Perry, J. C., 117–118
person schemas, 3–4, 6, 9, 115–117, 135
personal meaning systems, 9–10
personality, 1, 135
personalization, 100
physical movements, 65–66
Plutchik, R., 117–118
power struggles, 63–64
preconscious processing, 91–92, 135
primitive unconscious value, 86
problematic compromises, 135–136
procedural knowledge, 135
procrastination, 62–64
progress, evaluating, 9–10
projection, 103, 104–106, 135
projective identification, 103
pronoun stance, 45–46
protective compromises, 135–136
psychodynamic configuration, 135–136
Psychodynamic Diagnostic Manual, 19
psychoeducation, 67–68
psychological reactions, 65–66

rational views, 9–10
rationalization, 100
reaction formation, 100–101
realistic self-schemas, 34–35
reappraisals, 23
reasoned thinking, 80–81
reciprocal aggressor role, 79
reenactment scenarios, 41
reflective awareness, 10–11
reflective conscious awareness, 34
reflective functioning, parental, 22
reflective self-awareness, 10, 48, 49–50,
    82–83, 113
Reidbord, S. P., 117–118
relational model, 135–136
relationship attitudes, 6
relationship capacities, 65
    formulation and, 66–67
    observation and, 65–66
    summary of, 75
    technique and, 67–68, 71
        middle ground, 70–73
        narrating stories in new ways, 73–75
        new and old relationship patterns, 69–70
relationship patterns, 53
    formulation, 54–55
        excessive attention seeking and, 57
        excessive fear of abandonment and,
            55–56
        harsh inner critics and, 57–58
        observation and, 53–54
        passivity as attachment strategy, 56
        pathological self-soothing and, 57
        rivalry and, 57
        roles of self and, 55
        therapeutic alliances and, 55
    new and old, 69–70
    summary of, 64
    technique and, 58–59
        narcissism, 60–62
        passive-aggressive patterns, 59–60
        procrastination, 62–64
relationships, 51. *See also* role-relationship
    models
repetitive interpersonal patterns, 3
repetitive phenomena, 4, 5–6
representations, 135–136
repression, 102
reschematization, 135–136
retrospective traumas, 78–79
rivalry, 57
role reversal, 66–67, 103
role-playing scenarios, 33

role-relationship models (RRMs), 10–11, 17–18,
    46–47, 54, 83–84
    defensive, 55–56
    desired, 135–136
    dormant, 54
    dreaded, 135–136
    paranoid position and, 42
    procrastination and, 63–64
    relationship capacities and, 69
    relationship patterns and, 58
    sexual abuse and, 78–79, 80
    splitting and, 102–103
ruminative rehearsal, 34

safety, 7–8, 49–50
Saklofske, D. H., 117–118
Schafer, R., 8
schemas, 135–136. *See also* self-schemas
    person schemas, 3–4, 6, 9, 115–117, 135
secure attachment style, 21–22
self-appraisals, 20–21, 23, 84–86, 113
self-assertion, 56
self-attributions, 23
self-awareness, 81
    reflective, 10, 48, 49–50, 82–83, 113
self-coherence, 84–86
self-concept, 6, 25, 61, 122–123, 136
    degraded, 57–58
    developmental framework of, 21
self-confidence, 9–10
self-conscious thought, 81
self-control, 99
self-criticisms, 3–4, 20–21
self-degradation, 80
self-direction, 19
self-disgust, 39–42, 57–58
self-efficacy, 7
self-esteem, 15, 23, 25–26, 27–28, 58–59
self-evaluation, 10
self-governance, 84–86
self-image, 33–34, 101
self-judgments, 20–21, 34, 57–58
self-monitoring, 15
self-narratives, 23, 37, 69, 96
    formulation and
        self-disgust and, 39–42
        theory for, 42–43
    observation and, 37–38
        topics deserving more attention, 38–39
    parallel processing and, 48–49
    summary of, 49–50
    technique and, 43–45
        insight, 46–48

linking, 45
   patient's pronoun stance, 45–46
   reinforcing new narratives, 46
self-objects, 42, 136
self-observations, 27–28
self-organization, 13, 15, 136
   connectivity and, 25–26
   development of, 21–23
   formulation and, 17–20
   levels of integration, 18–19
   observation and, 16
   self-other formulation and, 20–21
   summary of, 26
   technique and, 23–24
   transference and, 24–25
self-other formulation, 20–21, 54
self-presentation, 16, 77
self-reflective awareness, 136
self-regard, 15
self-regulation, 99
self-sacrifice, 101
self-schemas, 17, 96, 136
   abandonment fears and, 55–56
   degraded, 34–35
   realistic, 34–35
   state and relationship cycle and, 30
   supraordinate, 136
self-soothing, pathological, 57
self-states, 17, 19, 27, 136
   dissociation and, 41
   formulation and, 29–31
   observing transitions and, 27–28
     over-modulated states, 28
     shimmering states, 29
     under-modulated states, 28
     well-modulated states, 28
   summary of, 35
   technique and, 31–32
   for safe emotional expression, 32–35
self-subordination, 39
self-talk, 45–46
separation anxiety, 21–22, 24–25, 30, 38
sexual abuse, 81–82
   in childhood, 78–79, 80
sexual desire, 78
sexual preferences, 77
sexual relationships, 77
   formulation and, 78–80
   observation and, 77
   summary of, 87
   technique and, 80–81, 84–87
     erotic transference and, 81–84
   therapeutic actions and, 85

shame, avoidances of, 94–96
shimmering states, 29, 40, 96–97, 120–121
Singer, J. L., 117–118
Skodol, A. E., 19
Slade, A., 22
splitting, 102–103
state and relationship cycle, 30
states of mind, 3–4, 9, 27–28, 136
   over-modulated, 4, 27, 28, 53–54
   shimmering, 29, 40, 96–97, 120–121
   under-modulated, 28, 82–83
   well-modulated, 28
Stinson, C. H., 117–118
stranger anxiety, 21
stress, 37–38, 92
   childhood and, 66–67
substance abuse, 57
sulking, 45–46
supportive listening, 55
supportive psychotherapy, 65
suppression, 102
supraordinate configurations, 17
supraordinate self-schema, 136
suspicious relationship patterns, 58

tense state of mind, 4
therapeutic alliance, 8–9, 10–11, 19–20, 67–68,
     82–83, 95–96, 136
   emotional avoidance maneuvers and, 110
   relationship patterns and, 55
   self-narratives and, 37, 41–42
   self-states and, 29, 31–32
   transference and, 24–25
time frames, 15, 37
topic selection, 110
topical triggers, 6–7
topics of concern, 3–4, 5–6, 9
   self-narratives and, 37
trains of thought, extreme, 96–97
transactive scenario, 17–18
transference, 6, 44, 55, 70–73, 86
   ambivalent feelings, 72
   counter-transference, 10–11, 31, 65–66, 136
   erotic, 81–84
   negative reactions, 65, 66
   positive reactions, 66
   self-organization and, 24–25
   self-states and, 29, 31–32
   therapeutic alliance and, 24–25
traumas
   in childhood, 41
   memory of, 92–93
   retrospective, 78–79

trial interventions, 15
trust, 66

unconditional positive regard, 55
unconscious emotional potentials, 91
    formulation and, 92–93
        linked associations, 93
    observation and, 91–92
    summary of, 98
    technique and, 93–94
        avoidance of shame, 94–96
        extreme trains of thought, 96–97
under-modulated states of mind, 28, 82–83
unemployment, 96–97

Vaillant, G., 117–118
verbal statements, 6, 25–26

verbalizations, 65–66
voyeurism, 80

Wachtel, P. L., 5
well-modulated states of mind, 28
Winnicott, D. W., 10, 41
wish-fear dilemma, 20–21, 30–31, 34, 47–48,
        55–56, 122–123
withdrawal, 33
working memory, 32
working model, 136
worst-case scenarios, 8

zealotry, 101
Zeidner, M., 117–118
Zimmerman, J., 19
Znoj, H., 117–118